Simply Super Bulletin Boards

Amy Vangsgard

Alleyside Press®

Fort Atkinson, Wisconsin

Published by Alleyside Press, an imprint of Highsmith Press LLC
Highsmith Press
W5527 Highway 106
P.O. Box 800
Fort Atkinson, Wisconsin 53538-0800
1-800-558-2110

© Amy Vangsgard, 1997
Cover design: Frank Neu

The paper used in this publication meets the minimum requirements of
American National Standard for Information Science — Permanence of
Paper for Printed Library Material. ANSI/NISO Z39.48-1992.

Library of Congress Cataloging-in-Publication Data

   Vangsgard, Amy.
     Simply super bulletin boards / Amy Vangsgard.
       p. cm.
     Includes bibliographical references (p.).
     ISBN 0-917846-89-3 (pbk. : alk. paper)
     1. Bulletin boards. I. Title.
   LB1043.58.V35 1997
   371.33'56–dc21   97-10561
                          CIP

Contents

Making Your Bulletin Boards Easy-to-Make and Easy-to-Do

Creating exciting bulletin boards can brighten up your entire library or classroom, calling attention to subjects you want to highlight. *Simply Super Bulletin Boards* includes festivals from around the world that will take your readers on a journey of exploration. You'll also find animal antics that will get your readers howling, hopping, leaping and purring for books. Have fun creating bulletin boards that are…*simply super!*

As you read through the suggestions here, keep in mind that each board is designed to work in a variety of situations. If your bulletin board proportions are different from the sample displays, use the tips offered in Design Basics (p. 6) to rearrange the pattern pieces for your setting. The general information below will help you get started creating effective and dramatic bulletin boards that are simple and inexpensive to make.

Bulletin board themes & patterns

Bulletin board patterns

Patterns for the individual elements of each bulletin board are provided so that you can mix and match pieces to create displays that fit your setting. Each element can be enlarged using an opaque or overhead projector; or following the drawings in the book, you can create your own patterns freehand. The number of elements you choose to use will be determined by the amount of space you have and the amount of time you have to create them.

Kids can make it!

There are fun, theme-related crafts that correspond with each of the bulletin boards. Getting kids involved is critical to creating memorable learning experiences and to motivating youngsters to read about each of the selected topics. These projects can be constructed as separate activities and then displayed on the bulletin board or hung around the room.

Directions for Kids Can Make It projects call for photocopying patterns on construction paper or card stock. Most photocopiers will be able to handle 8½" x 11" construction weight or heavier paper in their "top tray" or "direct feed" loader. These are the trays that are made to handle heavier papers, and should be used if reproducing patterns to heavier stocks.

Bulletin boards that display children's work

In addition to the "Kids Can Make It" projects, the bulletin board designs can be altered to display other forms or styles of work completed by children. For example, in the "Leaping Library Books," children can write book reports or poems about frogs on lily pads. These works can be arranged on the bulletin board in rows under a banner or next to the frog projects. With the "Las Posadas" bulletin board, children can make tiny piñatas and arrange them on the bulletin board in rows under a banner or pictures.

Table displays

You can share other materials on a topic which cannot be displayed on the bulletin board by creating a matching table display. Each theme includes some starter suggestions for books and items to display, and ways to arrange these materials that will spark any child's imagination.

To create the table displays, you will need the following materials:

- ❖ poster board
- ❖ clear packing tape
- ❖ scissors
- ❖ pencil
- ❖ yardstick

You can make a table display to match your bulletin board by following these directions:

1. Cut a 22" x 28" sheet of poster board in half, lengthwise. Cut one of the halves of poster board in half, widthwise.

2. Lay poster board sections flat on a table with the long section in the middle and short sections on opposite ends. Using clear packing tape, tape the ends of the longer section to the short sections, creating a foldout display.

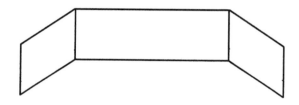

3. Staple or glue coordinating elements from the bulletin board to the table display.

4. To store, fold both sides inward.

Bookmarks

Children love to collect bookmarks, making them perfect for introducing a new subject, as well as reinforcing the joy of reading. In each chapter, there is a reproducible bookmark provided so you can give one to all of your eager readers.

Book lists for display suggestions

A book list is included with each chapter to assist you in your search for books which can be displayed or recommended to your readers.

Design basics

Composition

You want to create a composition that moves the viewer's eyes around the board and holds their interest. To do this, each of the bulletin board compositions provides a visual pathway for viewers to follow. The title, for instance, causes the eye to move from left to right. From there, the eye moves into and around the board. So before stapling the elements of your board in place, pin them up with straight pins. Then stand across the room and look at your composition. Does your eye get stuck? If so, make some adjustments and when it looks right, staple everything in place.

Here are a few basic principles that will make it easier for you to move elements to create visually exciting combinations.

A symmetrical composition, where the divisions are equal, appears static and without movement.

An asymmetrical composition with unequal divisions is more dynamic.

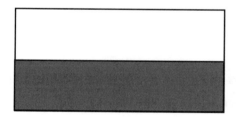

In this example, your eye moves from one corner to the other and gets stuck. The movement is limited.

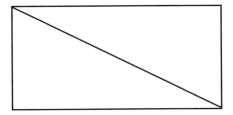

By using several diagonal lines, the eye is moved all around the page in continuous motion.

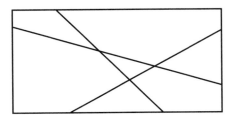

The rectangle in this composition has been placed in the center where it has become stagnant, without movement.

In this composition, the rectangle appears to be moving across the page because of its asymmetrical placement.

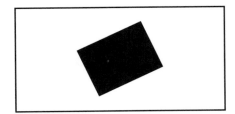

Colors and texture

Each bulletin board design suggests a color scheme. These colors were chosen for several reasons:

❖ Colors are selected to be analogous (in the same family) and to blend together in the composition;

❖ Colors that contrast add interest and emphasis. For example, green and red are opposites on the color wheel and they are often used next to each other to add contrast;

❖ Colors that contrast with each other (dark and light), can be especially effective when creating text in an easy-to-read banner;

❖ Colors that are themed or connected with the subject. For example, red and green are associated with Christmas; pastels are theme colors for Easter.

You can add a lot to the design and impact of your boards by using a variety of textures when selecting objects. For instance, items like colored tissue paper, aluminum foil, textured paint, corrugated paper and yarn are also easy to get and not expensive.

Time savers

Here are a few time-saving tips:

1. Choose fewer elements to make your composition. For example, in the "Kite Festival" there is a banner, two kites and two children. You can simplify this board by simply making the banner and one kite. If you don't want to make your own kite, you can buy a kite and pin it up as your artwork.

2. Many hands make light work. Have a group of children help color and cut out the different elements of your bulletin board.

3. Make a bulletin board of children's work and you only need to make the background and banner.

4. Stack papers and cut 2-3 items at the same time.

Storing bulletin boards to use again

Once you have created a beautiful bulletin board, you can save it—and save time next year!

1. Take a picture of each bulletin board. Store one set of photos in a picture file or photo album for further reference, and list the photos by title.

2. Remove the staples from the bulletin board. Then lay the flat elements on top of the background craft paper and roll the craft paper into a tube. Use a large rubber band to secure the tube. Now make a stronger storage container from an empty cardboard tube. (Ask a carpet store to save them for you.) You can cut carpet tubes down to size with a coping saw or a serrated knife. Make a cap for the bottom opening with masking tape to cover the hole or by gluing strips of paper across the opening. Write the title of the board on each tube.

3. To store thicker or three-dimensional elements or small loose pieces, create a storage portfolio for the objects by taking two sheets of poster board or cardboard that are the same size and tape them together on three sides. Label the outside of the portfolio.

Festivals Around the World

1 Kite Festival

Our affection for kites is as old as our dream of flying, and as universal. There are kite flying festivals in both Eastern and Western cultures. In the British Isles, for instance, kites are flown to celebrate "Michaelmas," the Feast of Saint Michael. Legends portray Saint Michael as a dragon slayer, who saved the village people from the forces of evil and destruction. Michaelmas coincides with the harvest, in early autumn.

In Eastern cultures, the Chinese Double Ninth Festival falls on the ninth day of the ninth lunar month. This holiday usually falls in January, and it is a joyful celebration of the forces of good. Legends dating back from the Han Dynasty tell of a wise clairvoyant who tried to warn his people of an impending disaster. Yet only one man would heed the warning. This man, known as Woon Ging, vowed to save the people of his village, but no one would listen to his pleas. Finally, Woon Ging led his family to the top of a high mountain to escape the disaster, wearing tiny pieces of dogwood and using kites to reach up to the heavens. A flood came and destroyed the village and all of its people. Only Woon Ging and his family managed to survive. To this day, it is considered good luck and a sign of good fortune to fly a kite from the top of a mountain on the Chinese Double Ninth Festival.

Directions for bulletin board (p.13)

BACKGROUND: Cover bulletin board by cutting light blue craft paper to size and stapling to the board. Cut a 12"-wide section of green craft paper the same length as bulletin board for the grass. Staple green craft paper to the bottom of the bulletin board.

BANNER: Enlarge banner onto bright yellow craft paper and outline letters and design with black, wide-tip felt pen. Using markers, color letters red and design green. Cut out banner and staple to bulletin board.

KITES: Enlarge kites onto yellow craft paper and outline with black, wide-tip felt marker. Use orange, red and green markers to color kites. Cut out kites. Cut ½" x 4" strips of yellow construction paper and glue to the back of dragon kite. Glue kite string to the back of dragon kite

Materials you need
- light blue craft paper for the background
- green craft paper for the grass
- bright yellow craft paper for the banner and kites
- white craft paper for the children
- yellow construction paper
- kite string or yarn
- black, red, orange, green and skin tone wide-tip, felt markers
- white glue

Tools you need
- opaque or overhead projector
- photocopy machine
- scissors
- stapler
- pins

to link sections together. Staple kites to bulletin board.

CHILDREN: Enlarge children onto white craft paper and outline with black, wide-tip felt marker. Using markers, color girl's dress and boy's pants red. Color hair and skin tones as desired. Staple kite string to each paper-child's hand and to his or her kite.

Kids can make it!

Enlarge owl kite and dragon kite onto separate 8½"x11" sheets of white paper. Photocopy kites onto white construction paper. Have children make kites by following directions for the bulletin board kites above. Create a bulletin board display of kites; or, using clothespins or metal clips, attach kites to a string stretched across the classroom or library.

Kite Festival bookmark

Photocopy bookmark onto light blue, yellow or red copier paper.

Foldout table display

Follow "Foldout Table Display" directions on pp. 5–6, using light blue poster board. Staple on dragon kite or other kites to create the display. Add books on kites, kite-making and kite festivals around the world such as those in the following list.

For display or further reading

The Dragon Kite. Nancy Luenn. Illustrated by Michael Hague. Orlando, FL: Harcourt, 1982. (o.p.)

The Emperor and the Kite. Jane Yolen. Cleveland, OH: World, 1967.

Festivals Together. Diana Carey and Judy Large. Hudson, NY: Hawthorn Press, 1993. 223p.

Fishing for Angels: The Magic of Kites. David Evans. Annick Press, 1991. Distributed by Firefly.

Games of the World: How to Make Them, How to Play Them, How They Came to Be. Frederic V. Grunfelf. Swiss Committee for UNICEF, 1975. 280 p.

Kites: Twelve Easy-to-Make High Fliers. Norma Dixon. New York: Beech Tree, 1996. 48 p.

Kites and Flying Objects. Denny Robson, Danbury, CT: Gloucester Press, 1992.

Kiteworks: Exploration in Kite Building and Flying. Maxwell Eden. New York: Sterling, 1991. 288p.

The Ultimate Kite Book. Paul and Helene Morgan. New York: Simon &Schuster, 1992. 80p.

Why Kites Fly: The Story of the Wind at Work. Don Dwiggins. Chicago: Children's Press, 1976.

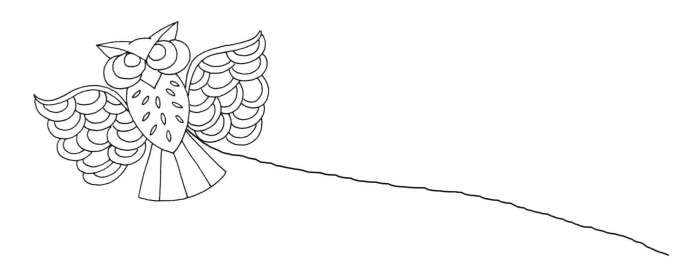

Kite Festival

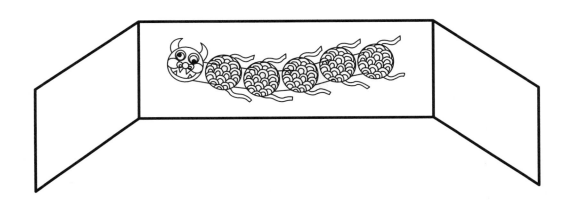

Kite Festival

2 Purim

Purim is a Jewish holiday that celebrates the victory of mercy over hatred and courage over fear. As recorded from ancient times in the "Megillah" (from the Book of Esther), there once lived a king names Xerxes, who lived in the land of Persia. The king had a wife, Queen Esther, who kept a secret from her husband. Esther was Jewish. Since Jews were not well-liked in Persia, the queen feared that telling Xerxes of her background would mean immediate banishment from Persia. Esther's cousin, Mordecai, was known to be Jewish, but he was well-liked by the king because Mordecai had once saved the king's life.

The king had a vizier or counselor named Haman. Haman believed everyone should bow to him as he took his walks through the city, but Mordecai refused to bow to the vizier, explaining that Jews did not bow to anyone or anything but their Lord. Mordecai's refusal infuriated Haman. The vizier decided not only to kill Mordecai, but all of the Jewish people in Persia. Mordecai begged Esther to save the Jews. Esther decided to invite Mordecai and Haman to a special feast with the king and discuss matters. But when the king learned that Haman was planning to kill Mordecai, along with all the Jews in Persia, Xerxes had Haman put to death.

Purim is celebrated during late February or early March. As the story of Purim is read from the Megillah, children are encouraged to yell, hiss, shout and use their special noisemakers to blot out the name "Haman" as it is read.

Directions for Bulletin Board (p. 17)

BACKGROUND: Cover bulletin board by cutting white craft paper to size and stapling to board.

BANNER: Glue a Styrofoam ball to each end of cardboard tubes and let dry. Paint cardboard tube and Styrofoam balls with bright blue paint and let dry. Cut a 1' x 6' banner from yellow craft paper. Enlarge banner design onto center of yellow banner paper and outline letters and design with black marker. Color in letters and designs with orange and green, wide-tip felt markers. Glue a blue cardboard tube to each end of yellow banner. Roll end of banner up to the edge of design and glue in place. Staple banner to bulletin board.

Materials you need
- white craft paper for the background
- bright yellow craft paper for the banner
- two 16" cardboard tubes (approx. 1½" in diameter)
- four 2" Styrofoam balls
- bright blue tempera paint
- black, light green, yellow, orange, skin tone and bright blue, wide-tip, felt markers
- white glue

Tools you need
- opaque or overhead projector
- photocopy machine
- scissors
- stapler
- pins
- 1" flat-tip brush

BORDER AND PURIM FIGURES: Enlarge border design and Purim figures onto bulletin board and outline with black wide-tip felt marker. Using black, light green, yellow, orange, skin tone and bright blue, wide-tip felt markers; color in designs.

Kids can make it!

Enlarge Purim figures onto an 8½" x 11" sheet of white paper. Photocopy figures onto white construction paper. Have children color and cut out figures. Glue figures to craft sticks to make "Purim Puppets."

Purim bookmark

Photocopy bookmark onto blue, orange or light green copier paper.

Foldout table display

Follow "Foldout Table Display" directions on pp. 5–6, using yellow or bright blue poster board. Enlarge Purim figures onto white poster board and outline with black, wide-tip felt markers. Using markers, color figures and then cut out. Staple Purim figures onto display. Use photos or examples of authentic artifacts, such as Jewish religious articles, crafts and/or musical instruments from Israel, or spring flowers to enhance display. Add books on Israel, the Jewish people, Jewish holidays, folk tales, arts, crafts and cooking of the Jewish people such as those in the following list.

For display or further reading

Celebrate: A Book of Jewish Holidays. Judith Gross. New York: Platt and Munk, 1992.

The Children's Jewish Holiday Kitchen. Joan Nathan. New York: Schocken, 1987. 144p.

Festival of Esther: The Story of Purim. Maida Silverman. Old Tappan, NJ: Simon & Schuster, 1989.

Festivals Together. Diana Carey and Judy Large. Hudson, NY: Hawthorn Press, 1993. 223p.

Fun with Jewish Rhymes. Sylvia Ross. New York: UAHC Press, 1992.

Jewish Holiday Fun. Judith Hoffman Corwin. Morristown, NJ: Silver Burdett, 1987. 64p.

Jewish Holidays. Mary Turch. New York: Crestwood House, 1990.

The Passover Journey. Barbara Diamond Goldin. New York: Viking Childrens Books, 1994. 64p.

Purim. Miriam Nerlove. Morton Grove, IL: Albert Whitman & Co., 1992.

The Treasury of Jewish Folklore. Nathan Ausubel. New York: Crown, 1989.

PURIM

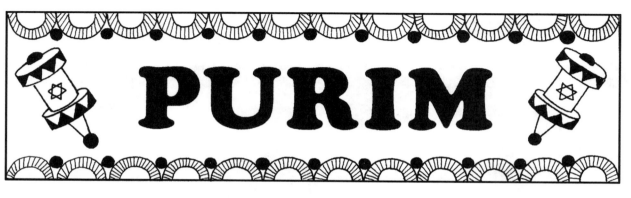

PURIM

3 Holi

Holi is a fun-filled holiday celebrated in late February or early March, during the harvest of wheat and mustard throughout India. The night before Holi, a large bonfire is made, known as the "burning of Holika." Holika represents evil, and the bonfire celebrates the victory of good over evil. Pine nuts and chick peas are roasted in the fire.

The next day is also called the "Festival of Color." As part of the festivities, celebrants "play" Holi with buckets of brightly colored powder or water: yellow, red, orange and green, which are used to cover or drench both friends and foes. People wear old clothes all day and by evening, everyone is dressed very "colorfully."

Throwing colored water is part of a custom derived from the playful stories of Krishna and Radha, who splashed each other in the river Yamura when enjoying the fresh spring weather. In the classroom or community hall, colored confetti paper makes for a good substitute.

Directions for bulletin board (p. 21)

BACKGROUND: Cover bulletin board by cutting green craft paper to size and stapling to board.

BANNER: Enlarge banner onto yellow craft paper and outline letters and design with black, wide-tip felt pen. Color in letters with green marker and designs with red, orange and green markers. Cut out banner and staple to bulletin board.

CHILDREN: Enlarge children onto white craft paper and outline with black, wide-tip felt marker. Using markers, color hair and skin as desired and design on clothing red, yellow, orange or green. Cut out children and staple to board.

CONFETTI: Stack yellow, orange and red construction paper and cut into ¼"-wide strips. Cut each color of strips into separate piles of small confetti squares. Using a glue stick, glue confetti

Materials you need
- bright green craft paper for the background
- bright yellow craft paper for the banner
- white craft paper for children
- yellow, orange and red construction paper
- black, green, red, orange, yellow and skin tone wide-tip felt markers
- pencil
- white glue stick

Tools you need
- opaque or overhead projector
- photocopy machine
- scissors
- stapler
- pins

to bulletin board. Each child should be spraying one color.

Kids can make it!

Give each child a sheet of white construction paper. Have children make drip drops of red, yellow, orange and green tempera paint on their paper. (Eye droppers or loaded paint brushes will work.) Using a drinking straw, children can then blow on drops to create splatter designs.

Holi bookmark

Photocopy bookmark onto green, yellow or orange copier paper.

Foldout table display

Follow "Foldout Table Display" directions on pp. 5–6, using green poster board. Staple a child throwing confetti on the display. Glue confetti on the display. Use photos or examples of artifacts from India, including wood or brass figures, fabrics, and/or baskets. Add books on India, holidays of the Indian people, folktales, arts, crafts and cooking of India, spring festivals from around the world such as those in the following list.

For display or further reading

Favorite Fairy Tales Told in India. Virginia Haviland. New York: Beech Tree Books, 1994. 96p.

Festivals Together. Diana Carey and Judy Large. Hudson, NY: Hawthorn Press, 1993. 223p.

Folk Tales of India. Brenda E.F. Beck. Chicago: University of Chicago Press, 1989.

Hindu Festivals. Holidays & Festivals series. Swasti Mitter. Vero Beach, Fla. : Rourke Enterprises, 1989.

The Hindu World. Patricia Bahree. Religions of the World Series. Trafalgar Sq.: David & Charles, 1989.

Indian Fairy Tales. Joseph Jacobs. Columbia, MO: South Asian Books, 1995.

Projects for Spring and Holiday Activities. Celia McInnes. Ada, OK: Garrett.

Seasons of Splendor: Tales, Myths and Legends of India. Madhur Jaffrey. New York: Atheneum, 1985.

Spring Festivals. Mike Rosen. New York: Bookwright Press, 1991.

A Taste of India. Roz Denny. New York: Thomson Learning, 1994. 48p.

4 Lei Day

In the Hawaiian Islands, May Day is Lei Day. While most of the world celebrates spring with bouquets of flowers, Hawaiians celebrate spring with beautiful flower necklaces, known as *leis* (pronounced "lays"). On this day, leis are given as gifts. There are numerous festivals in the islands, which include traditional Hawaiian music, hula dancing and the crowning of the Lei Day Queen. There are also numerous lei contests. Kapiolani Park in Honolulu hosts the state's largest lei contest.

Leis are seen everywhere in Hawaii. Recognized as a symbol of the islands, they are traditionally presented to friends as an expression of *aloha* (love, greetings, welcome and farewell) and are often given when someone is arriving for a visit or leaving on a trip. Many leis are simple strings of small orchids or carnations. Others are truly works of art and extremely valuable. The rarest and most expensive leis are made of feathers or tiny shells. On special ceremonies, important guests are presented with maile leis. These are long, open-ended strands of braided leaves of the maile plant, which has a spicy aroma.

Directions for bulletin board (p. 25)

BACKGROUND: Cover bulletin board by cutting blue craft paper to size and stapling to board.

BANNER: Enlarge banner onto beige craft paper and outline letters and design with black, wide-tip felt pen. Using markers, color letters green and flowers red and pink. Cut out banner and staple to bulletin board.

SAND: Cover bottom section of bulletin board by cutting beige craft paper to fit and staple to bulletin board.

PALM TREES: Enlarge tree trunks onto brown craft paper and outline design in black marker. Cut out tree trunks and staple to board. Enlarge palm fronds onto green craft paper and outline with black, wide-tip felt marker. Cut out palm fronds and fringe edges. Staple to bulletin board.

Materials you need

- bright blue craft paper for the background
- beige or white craft paper for the banner and sand
- white craft paper for the dancers
- green craft paper for the palm fronds
- brown craft paper for the tree trunks
- pink and red tissue paper
- green construction paper for the skirts
- black, pink, red and green and skin tone wide-tip, felt markers
- white glue

Tools you need

- opaque or overhead projector
- photocopy machine
- scissors
- stapler
- pins

Dancers: Enlarge dancers onto white craft paper and outline with black, wide-tip felt marker. Using markers, color skirt green, blouse red and leis pink. Color hair and skin as desired. Stack tissue paper and trace flower pattern onto top sheet. Cut out flowers and glue to leis. Enlarge skirt onto green craft paper. Cut out skirts and fringe the bottoms. Glue skirt onto dancers. Staple dancers to bulletin board.

Kids can make it!

Using flower pattern, cut out flowers from pink, red, white or yellow tissue paper. (Cutting through three layers of tissue at once will make it go faster.) Punch a hole in the center of each flower. Cut drinking straws into 1" sections. Cut a piece of string or yarn about 30" in length. String a straw piece first and knot the yarn around it, so the pieces don't fall off while stringing. String the straw pieces, putting three paper flowers between each section of straw. Knot the ends to create the lei.

Lei Day bookmark

Photocopy bookmark onto red, pink or green copier paper.

Foldout table display

Follow "Foldout Table Display" directions on pp. 5–6, using beige or blue poster board. Staple dancers onto the display. Use photos or examples of artifacts, such as leis, grass mats, carved bowls/utensils and/or musical instruments. Add books on Hawaii, the history of the Hawaiian Islands, folktales, arts and crafts of the Hawaiian people such as those in the following list.

For display or further reading

Luka's Quilt. Georgia Guback. New York: Greenwillow, 1994.

Honolulu. John Penisten. Morristown, NJ: Silver Burdett, 1990. 288p.

The Last Princess: The Story of Princess Ka'iulani of Hawai'i. Fay Stanley. New York: Four Winds, 1991.

Modern Hawaiian History. Ann Rayson. Honolulu, HI: Bess Press, 1984. 288p.

Raising Cane: The World of Plantation. Ronald Takaki. New York: Chelsea House. 1993. 125p.

Projects for Spring and Holiday Activities. Celia McInnes. Ada, OK: Garrett.

Spring Festivals. Mike Rosen. New York: Bookwright Press, 1991.

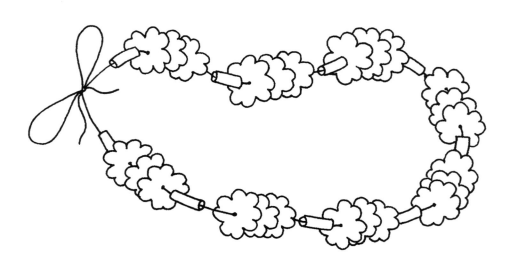

LEI DAY

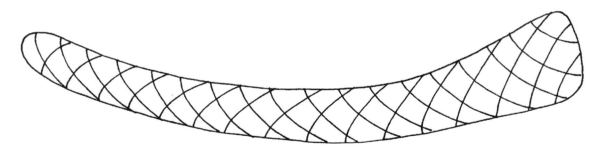

5 Hina Matsuri

The Japanese celebrate two doll festivals each year. The "Girls' Festival" is celebrated on March 3; May 5 is the "Boys' Festival." Both are part of the traditional "Hina Matsuri," where youngsters all over the country set up elaborate displays of their families' historical doll collections. Children dress in their best kimonos (a wide-sleeved Japanese robe, tied with a sash at the waist). When family and friends come to see the display, the youngsters offer them specially made tea and cakes.

The Girls' Festival dolls are displayed on steps. The top step, or the place of honor, is used for the Emperor or Empress. The steps below are for other members of the noble class. The dolls are passed from generation to generation and each is beautifully painted and dressed in true-to-life costumes. Flowers and food are displayed among the dolls as gifts. The Boys' Festival displays historical figures and warriors. Both festivals help youngsters learn more about Japanese history and culture.

Directions for Bulletin Board (p. 29)

BACKGROUND: Cover bulletin board by cutting red craft paper to size and stapling to board.

BANNER: Enlarge banner onto yellow craft paper and outline letters and design with black, wide-tip felt pen. Color in letters and design with black marker. Cut out banner and staple to bulletin board.

SHELVES: Cut 3"-wide strips from black craft paper. Staple black strips of craft paper to bulletin board to form shelves.

DOLLS: Enlarge dolls onto white craft paper and outline with black, round-tip felt marker. Using markers, color hair black, leave faces white and clothes yellow, light green, red and white. Cut out dolls and staple to board.

Materials you need
- red craft paper for the background
- yellow craft paper for the banner
- black craft paper for the shelves
- white craft paper for the dolls
- pencil
- black, red, yellow and light green wide-tip, felt markers
- black, round-tip felt marker

Tools you need
- opaque or overhead projector
- photocopy machine
- scissors
- stapler
- pins

Kids can make it!

Enlarge dolls onto separate 8½" x 11" sheets of white paper. Photocopy dolls onto white construction paper. Have children color their dolls with crayons; or paste pieces of fabric or wallpaper onto dolls. Cut out dolls and display on bulletin board.

Hina Matsuri bookmark

Photocopy bookmark onto red, white or yellow copier paper.

Foldout table display

Follow "Foldout Table Display" directions on pp. 5–6, using red poster board. Staple dolls to the display. Exhibit a collection of dolls from Japan and other items from traditional Japanese attire and/or artifacts. Display dolls from the United States and from around the world. Add books on Japan, Japanese customs and traditions, Japanese holidays, folktales and crafts of Japan; collecting and making dolls such as those in the following list.

For display or further reading

A to Zen: A Book of Japanese Culture. Ruth Wells. New York: Picture Book Studio, 1992.

Easy-to-Make Cloth Dolls and All the Trimmings. Jodie Davis. Charlotte, VT: Williamson Publishing Co., 1990. 224p.

Festivals of Japan. Hal Buell. Carson, CA: Books Nippan, 1985. 192p.

From Head to Toe: How a Doll is Made. Susan Kuklin. New York: Hyperion, 1994.

The How-to Book of International Dolls: A Comprehensive Guide to Making, Costuming, and Collecting Dolls. Loretta Holz. New York: Crown, 1980.

In the Eyes of the Cat: Japanese Poetry for All Seasons. Demi. Translated by Tze-si Huang. New York: Holt, 1992.

Red Dragonfly on My Shoulder. Sylvia Cassedy and Kunihiro Suetake, trans. Illustrated by Molly Bang. New York: HarperCollins, 1992.

Shizuko's Daughter. Kyoko Mori. New York: Holt, 1993. 240p.

A Taste of Japan. Jenny Pridgwell. New York: Thomson Learning, 1993. 48p.

Tree of Cranes. Allen Say. New York: Houghton Mifflin, 1991.

Hina Matsuri

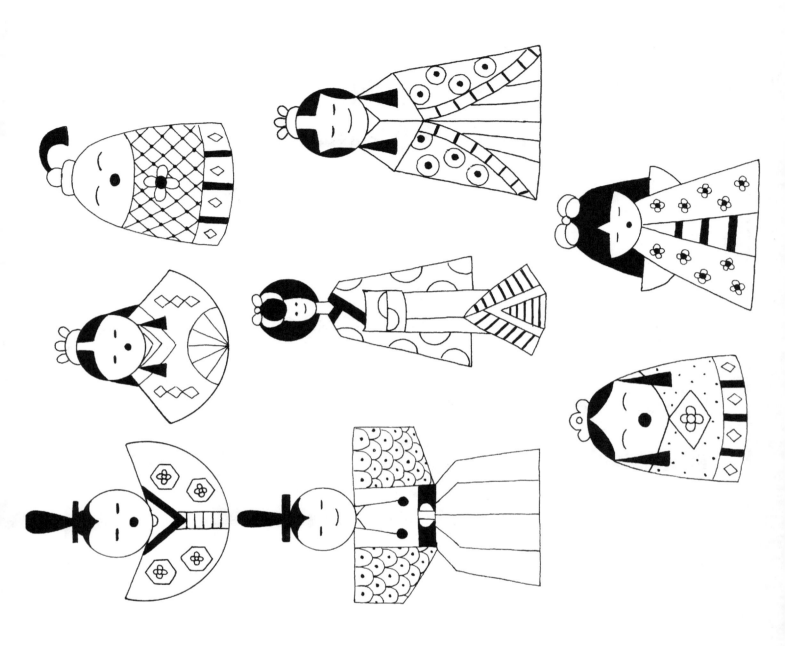

Hina Matsuri

6 Dragon Boat Festival

The Chinese first began "Dragon Boat Races" almost 3,000 years ago in the province of Hunan. According to legend, the townspeople of this province were celebrating the summer solstice. But the minister of the ruling class, a poet named Ch'u Yuan, was despondent. He was upset with the corrupt government and its failure to meet the needs of the townspeople. Seeing no way to correct the problems of Hunan, Ch'u Yuan jumped into the Mi Lo River and to his death. The sinister emperor was so moved by Ch'u Yuan's sacrifice that he soon corrected the ways of the Hunan government.

In the years that followed, Ch'u Yuan's death was remembered by "Dragon Boat" teams, racing to be the first to feed rice to the spirit of the drowned poet. To keep the rice from being eaten by water serpents, the rice was wrapped in bamboo leaves and tied with multi-colored string. Ch'u Yuan's followers believed that the rhythmic thrashing of the oars would frighten away fish that might eat the body of the revered statesman.

Today, Dragon Boat Races provide a joyous, festive atmosphere to honor the timeless values of the ancient Chinese culture.

Directions for Bulletin Board (p. 33)

BACKGROUND: Cover bulletin board by cutting yellow craft paper to size and stapling to board.

BANNER: Enlarge banner onto light blue craft paper. Outline and fill in letters and designs with black, wide-tip felt marker. Cut out banner and staple to bulletin board.

WATER: Enlarge water onto light blue craft paper. Outline design in black, wide-tip felt marker. Cut water the same width as board and staple to bulletin board.

DRAGON BOATS: Enlarge dragon boats onto white craft paper and outline with black, wide-tip felt marker. Using markers, color dragon boats red, yellow, light green, white and black. Cut out dragon boats and staple to board.

Materials you need
- bright yellow craft paper for the background
- light blue craft paper for the water and banner
- white craft paper for the dragon boats
- pencil
- black, red, yellow and light green wide-tip, felt markers

Tools you need
- opaque or overhead projector
- photocopy machine
- scissors
- stapler
- pins

Kids can make it!

Enlarge dragon boat onto an 8½" x 11" sheet of white paper. Photocopy dragon boat onto white construction paper. Have children color and cut out dragon boats. Glue dragon boats to craft sticks to make "dragon boat puppets." Display dragon boats on bulletin board to make an exciting boat race scene or have a relay race with dragon boat puppets.

Dragon Boat bookmark

Photocopy bookmark onto blue, yellow or red copier paper.

Foldout table display

Follow "Foldout Table Display" directions on pp. 5–6, using light blue poster board. Enlarge water design onto display and outline design with black, wide-tip felt marker. Staple dragon boats to display.

Display books on boat racing, boat building, boat artifacts, dragon boat races, China, Chinese history, holidays, folktales, arts, crafts and cooking such as those in the following list.

For display or further reading

Cat and Rat: The Legend of the Chinese Zodiac. Ed Young. New York: Holt, 1995.

Chinese Children's Stories. Emily Ching. Wonder Kids, 1991.

Cooking the Chinese Way. Ling Yu. Minneapolis, MN: Lerner Group, 1982. 48p.

The Craft of Sail. Jan Adkins. New York: Walker, 1984. 64p.

Distant Fires. Scott Anderson. Duluth, MN: Pfiefer-Hamilton, 1990. 176p.

The Folklore of World Holidays. Margaret Read MacDonald. Detroit: Gale, 1992.

Night Visitors. Retold by Ed Young. New York: Philomel, 1995.

Red Eggs and Dragon Boats: Celebrating Chinese Festivals. Carol Stepanchuk. Berkeley, CA: Pacific View Press, 1993. 48p.

The Seventh Sister: A Chinese Legend. Cindy Chang. Mahwah, NJ: Troll, 1994.

Tiki Tiki Tembo. Arlene Mozel. Illustrated by Blair Lent. New York: Holt, 1968. 48p.

Dragon Boat Festival

Dragon Boat Festival

7 Eid-ul-Fitr

Islam, a religion that stems from the Middle East and is now also observed in East Asia, India and Pakistan, has five pillars or basic principles: (1) the belief in one god, Allah; (2) prayers, or *Namaz*, are to be performed five times a day; (3) followers must make a pilgrimage or journey to Mecca, the homeland; (4) charity or *Zakat* must always be observed; and (5) those who believe in Islam must fast for an entire month during Ramadan, the ninth month of the Islamic calendar. Since the Islamic calendar is lunar, all new months begin with the sighting of the moon.

Eid-ul-Fitr celebrates the end of Ramadan. The holiday can only start if the new moon of the tenth month is sighted, which may not be visible until very late into the night. While waiting for the new moon, followers prepare for the celebration by laying out new clothes, wrapping presents and painting their hands and feet with the traditional Mehndi designs. Once religious leaders sight the new moon, the festivities of Eid-ul-Fitr begin. In the United States, the holiday lasts one day, but in the Middle East, Eid-ul-Fitr lasts up to three days.

Directions for Bulletin Board (p. 37)

BACKGROUND: Cover bulletin board by cutting dark blue craft paper to size and stapling to board.

BORDER: Cut 4"-wide strips of pink craft paper, long enough to cover the entire perimeter of the bulletin board. Enlarge border pattern onto strips of pink craft paper. Outline and fill in design with red, wide-tip felt marker. Staple strips of pink craft paper to bulletin board.

MOON AND TITLE: Enlarge moon and Eid ul-Fitr title onto white craft paper. Outline and fill in letters with red, wide-tip felt marker. Cut out moon and staple to bulletin board.

MEHNDI HANDS: Enlarge Mehndi hands onto pink craft paper and outline designs with a red, round-tip felt marker. Cut out hands and staple to bulletin board.

Materials you need

- dark blue craft paper for the background
- light pink craft paper for the border and hands
- white craft paper for the moon
- pencil
- red wide-tip, felt marker
- red round-tip, felt marker

Tools you need

- opaque or overhead projector
- photocopy machine
- scissors
- stapler
- pins

Kids can make it!

Have children trace their own hands onto pink or tan construction paper. Children can draw Mehndi designs onto their outlined hands with red, round-tip felt marker or red crayon. Cut out hands and display on bulletin boards.

Mehndi Hands bookmark

Photocopy bookmark onto pink or white copier paper.

Foldout table display

Follow "Foldout Table Display" directions on pp. 5–6, using dark blue poster board. Staple Mehndi hands onto board. Use photos or examples of artifacts from Islamic countries, such as brass figures, fabrics, and/or jewelry. Add books on the Middle East, Islam, Islamic holidays, folktales, arts, crafts and cooking of the Middle East such as those in the following list.

For display or further reading

The Arabian Knights Entertainments. Andrew Lang. Illustrated by Ford Schocken. New York: Dover, 1969. 424p.

The Children of Egypt. Matti A. Pitkänen. Minneapolis: Carolrhoda, 1991.

The Complete Middle East Cookbook. Tess Mallas. Boston, MA: C. E. Tuttle, 1993. 384p.

The Day of Ahmed's Secret. Florence Parry Heide and Judith Heide Gilliland. New York: Lothrop, Lee & Shepard, 1990.

Festivals Together. Diana Carey and Judy Large. Hudson, NY: Hawthorn Press, 1993. 223p.

Folktales of Egypt. Hasan El-Shamy. Chicago: Chicago Press, 1982.

The Land and People of Pakistan. Land and People series. Mark Weston. New York: HarperCollins.

Middle Eastern Food and Drink. Christine Osborne. Bookwright, 1988.

Muslim Festivals. Holidays & Festivals series. M.M. Ahsan. Vero Beach, FL : Rourke Ent., 1987.

The Muslim World. Richard Tames. Morristown, NJ: Silver Burdett, 1985. 48 pp.

Ramadan and Id Al-Fitr. Dianne MacMillan. Hillside, NJ: Enslow Publishers, 1994.

Two Pairs of Shoes. P.L. Travers. Illustrated by Leo and Diane Dillon. New York: Atheneum, 1980.

Eid-ul-Fitr

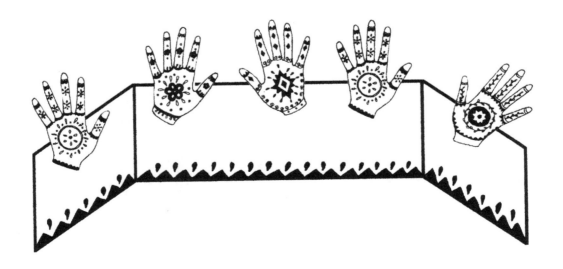

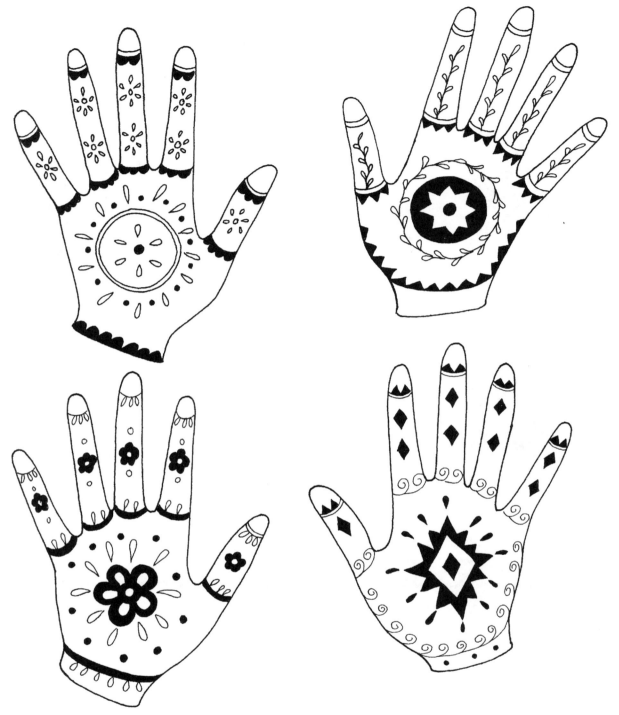

Eid-ul-Fitr

8 Las Posadas

The nine days before Christmas have special importance in Mexico and in Mexican American communities in the U.S. These days are called *posadas*, which means "inns" or "lodgings." On each day, parishioners reenact Mary and Joseph's search for lodgings on the first Christmas Eve.

During the days of "Las Posadas" children walk in procession dressed as angels or shepherds. The children travel from door to door in a neighborhood or village, singing the verses of the *letania* (the traditional posadas song). They carry small statues representing Mary and Joseph along with them.

The procession starts after dark, and people carry candles, *faroles* (paper lanterns), and banners. Those behind the doors of the first couple houses refuse the request for lodging by singing their own song. It is only after determined efforts on the part of the children (as did Mary and Joseph) that they finally are granted shelter. The occupants of the last house open the door and ask the worshippers to enter their home. Here there is a party, celebrated with plenty of delicious food and a piñata. The piñata, filled with candy and small gifts, is hung from the ceiling, and the children take turns trying to break it with a stick while blindfolded. The piñata can be raised or lowered, which makes for more fun.

Directions for Bulletin Board (p. 41)

BACKGROUND: Cover bulletin board by cutting yellow craft paper to size and stapling to board.

BANNER: Enlarge banner onto pink craft paper and outline letters with green, wide-tip felt pen. Paint in letters with green tempera. Cut out banner and staple to bulletin board. Cut a 4"-wide strip from red construction paper, and fringe by making 2" cuts every ½" along one side of the red strip. Cut red, fringed strip to the same height as the banner. Staple fringed strip to each end of the banner. You may need more than one fringed strip.

DONKEY PIÑATA: Enlarge donkey piñata onto white craft paper and cut out. Cut 2"-wide strips from white, green and pink construction paper. Fringe by making 1" cuts every ½" along one side of each strip. (You can stack strips and cut several at one time.) Starting from the bottom of

Materials you need
- bright yellow craft paper for background
- bright pink craft paper for the banner
- white craft paper for the children
- red, white, pink and green construction paper
- green and black and skin tone wide-tip, felt markers
- white glue
- green tempera paint
- yarn or thin rope
- red and green curl ribbon
- small, individually wrapped candies

Tools you need
- opaque or overhead projector
- photocopy machine
- scissors
- stapler
- pins
- 1" flat-tip brush
- ¼" round-tip brush

the piñata, cut strips the same width as piñata. Glue strips in alternating rows of color onto the piñata. Cut ½"-wide strips of red construction paper and glue onto donkey's head to make a bridle and tail. Cut a 1" circle from green construction paper for eye; and a 1½" circle out of red construction paper for the bridle. Glue the circles onto donkey's head. Staple piñata onto bulletin board.

CHILDREN: Enlarge patterns of children onto white craft paper and outline with black, wide-tip felt marker. Using markers, color hair and skin as desired. Leave boys' clothing white and color trim red or green. Leave girls' blouses white; color skirts red or pink and color trim green. Make bat green. Cut out children and staple to bulletin board.

RIBBON AND CANDY: Cut ribbon into 12" lengths and curl with scissors. Staple curled ribbon and wrapped candies onto bulletin board.

Kids can make it!

Enlarge donkey piñata onto an 8½" x 11" sheet of white paper. Photocopy donkey piñata onto white construction paper. Have children decorate their piñatas by following directions from above. Create a bulletin board display of piñatas or suspend piñatas from ceiling with strings.

Las Posadas bookmark

Photocopy bookmark onto pink, green, yellow or red copier paper.

Foldout table display

Follow "Foldout Table Display" directions on pp. 5–6, using yellow poster board. Staple a donkey piñata, curled ribbon and candies onto the display. Use authentic artifacts, such as a serape or sombrero, to enhance the display. Add books on Mexico; Latin America; Christmas around the world; or Mexican folktales such as those in the following list.

For display or further reading

Carlos, Light the Farolito. Jean Ciavonne. Illustrated by Donna Clair. New York: Clarion, 1995.

Christmas Around the World. Emily Kelley. Illustrated by Priscilla Kiedrowski. Minneapolis, MN: Lerner, 1986. 48p.

Count Your Way Through Mexico. Jim Haskins. Minneapolis, MN: Lerner, 1989. 24 pp.

Feliz Nochebuena Feliz Navidad, Christmas Feasts of the Hispanic Caribbean. Maricel Presilla. New York: Holt, 1994.

Fiesta! Mexico's Great Celebrations. Elizabeth Silverthorne. Brookfield, CT: Millbrook Press, 1992.

Fiesta USA. George Ancona. New York: Dutton, 1995.

Indo-Hispanic Folk Art Traditions, Christmas and Other Year-Round Activities. Bobbi Salinas. Oakland, CA: Piñata Publications, 1987.

Las Navidades: Popular Christmas Songs from Latin America. Selected by Lulu Delacre. New York: Scholastic, 1990.

Nine Days to Christmas. Marie Hall Ets. New York: Puffin, 1991. (1960 Caldecott Award.)

Piñata Maker/ El Piñatero. George Ancona. Orlando, FL: Harcourt Brace, 1994.

Piñatas and Paper Flowers: Holidays of the Americas in English and Spanish. Bilingual ed. Lila Perl. Spanish version by Alma Flor Ada. New York: Clarion, 1983.

LAS POSADAS

9 Saint Lucia Day

The Christmas season in Sweden, and in Swedish communities throughout the world, begins on December 13 with *Luciadagen* or Saint Lucia Day. The holiday commemorates the generous spirit of Saint Lucia, a young girl who lived in Sicily about A.D. 300 and who saved the Swedish people from starvation. According to legend, Sweden was in the grip of a terrible famine when Saint Lucia miraculously arrived in a large ship, her head circled in light, laden with food and clothing. (The name "Lucia" means light.)

Today, Luciadagen is celebrated in homes throughout Sweden. At dawn, the eldest daughter, who represents Lucia, dresses in a white gown with a red sash. She wears a crown of greens topped by real candles. Singing the traditional Italian melody, *Santa Lucia*, she is followed by her younger sisters, also in white gowns and red sashes. Boys also participate in the celebration, wearing white gowns and white, cone-shaped hats—decorated with gold stars.

The oldest daughter caries a tray of coffee and festive Lucia buns, generously feeding her family as did the patron Lucia hundreds of years ago. The buns, especially baked with saffron flavoring, have many traditional shapes. The most common are the Lussekatter or "Lucia cats." A good-luck symbol since ancient times, the cat was a sign to keep the devil out of the house.

Directions for Bulletin Board (p. 45)

BACKGROUND: Cover bulletin board by cutting blue craft paper to size and stapling to board.

BANNER: Enlarge banner onto yellow craft paper and outline letters and design with black, wide-tip felt marker. Using markers, color letters and berries red and holly green. Cut out banner and staple to bulletin board.

CHILDREN: Enlarge children onto white craft paper and outline with black, wide-tip felt marker. Using markers, pointed hat white with yellow stars, wreaths green with red berries and candle flames yellow. Glue yellow yarn on hair. Cut out children and glue hats on their heads. Staple children to bulletin boards.

SWEDISH HEARTS: Enlarge heart pattern onto an 8½" x 11" white sheet of paper. Photocopy heart

Materials you need

- bright blue craft paper for the background
- bright yellow craft paper for the banner
- white craft paper for the children
- red and white construction paper for hearts
- pencil
- black, yellow, green ,red, blue and skin tone wide-tip, felt markers
- white glue
- yellow yarn

Tools you need

- opaque or overhead projector
- photocopy machine
- scissors
- stapler
- pins

pattern onto white and red construction paper. Cut out heart patterns and cut along dotted lines. Weave one red heart pattern with one white heart pattern as seen in figure 1 below. Glue ends together. Staple Swedish hearts to bulletin board.

Kids can make it!

Enlarge hat with candles onto an 8½" x 11" sheet of white paper. Photocopy hat with candles onto white construction paper. Have children color and cut out hats. Punch a hole in each end of the hat and tie a 12"-length of yarn to each hole. Tie hats onto children's heads. Children can also make Swedish hearts.

Saint Lucia bookmark

Photocopy bookmark onto red, yellow or green copier paper.

Foldout table display

Follow "Foldout Table Display" directions on pp. 5–6, using bright blue poster board. Staple children with hats onto the display. Use authentic artifacts, such as Scandinavian Christmas decorations, Advent wreaths, candleholders, small Christmas tree or pine bows to enhance display. Add books on Christmas around the world, Scandinavia, Scandinavian crafts, customs and cooking, Scandinavian folktales and Norse mythology such as those in the following list.

For display or further reading

Christmas Around the World. Emily Kelley. Illustrated by Priscilla Kiedrowski. Minneapolis, MN: Lerner, 1986. 48p.

Christmas Trolls. Jan Brett. New York: Putnam, 1993. 32p.

Favorite Fairy Tales Told in Sweden. Virginia Havilland. New York: Morrow, 1994. 72p.

Norse Gods and Giants. Ingrid and Edgar D'Aulaires. New York: Doubleday, 1967.

The Sleepy Baker. Christin Drake. Flagstaff, AZ: Northland, 1993. 56p.

Super Grandpa. David Schwartz. Illustrated by Bert Dodson. New York: Lothrop, 1991.

Victorian Family Celebrations. Sarah Ban Breathnach. New York: Fireside, 1992. 224p.

Waiting for Christmas Stories. Bethany Roberts. New York: Clarion, 1994.

The Whole Christmas Catalogue for Kids. Louise Betts. New York: Mallard Press, 1988.

The Wild Christmas Reindeer. Jan Brett. New York: Putnam, 1990. 32p.

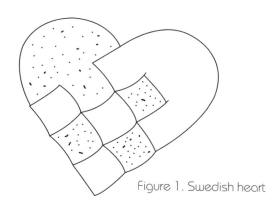

Figure 1. Swedish heart

St. Lucia Day

St. Lucia Day

10 Kwanzaa

Kwanzaa is an African American holiday based on the traditional African festival of the harvest of the first crops. It starts on December 26 and lasts for seven days. The holiday centers around the Nguzo Saba, the seven principles of Black culture, developed in 1966 by M. Ron Karenga, a professor of Pan-African studies. These principles are: Umoja (unity); Kujichagulia (self-determination); Ujima (collective work and responsibility); Ujamaa (cooperative economics); Nia (purpose); Kuumba (creativity); and Imani (faith).

Together, these principles form the character of the African American culture and the lessons of the holiday are taught every year. Each day of Kwanzaa is dedicated to understanding and dedicating oneself to one of the seven principles, as family members light one of the seven candles in the Kinara (candleholder). Near the end of the holiday, the community gathers for a feast, with music and dancing, called Karamu. Everyone sips juice from the Kikombe Cha Umoja, a large goblet or cup that symbolizes staying together. There is also a special flag that is raised, the "Bendera ya Taifa," which symbolizes the pride of the African American people.

Directions for Bulletin Board (p. 49)

BACKGROUND: Cover bulletin board by cutting yellow craft paper to size and stapling to board.

BANNER: Enlarge banner onto red craft paper and outline letters and design with black, wide-tip felt pen. Color in letters and design with black markers. Cut out banner and staple to bulletin board.

KINARA (candleholder): Enlarge candle pattern onto red and green poster board and outline with black, wide-tip felt marker. Make three red candles and four green candles. Using black marker, color in designs and one of the green candles. Cut out candles. Fold candles back along dotted lines. Fit the tab into the slit in the base. Arrange candles on the bulletin board in the form of a Kinara. Staple black candle in the center, three green candles on the left and three red candles on the right.

Materials you need
- bright yellow craft paper for the background
- red craft paper for the banner
- red and green 2-ply poster board for candles and corn
- pencil
- black wide-tip, felt markers
- white glue
- popcorn (unpopped)

Tools you need
- opaque or overhead projector
- photocopy machine
- scissors
- stapler
- pins

VIBUNZI (ears of corn): "Vibunzi" represents children. Enlarge ears of corn onto green poster board and outline with black, wide-tip felt marker. Cut out ears of corn. Glue popcorn to ears of corn and let dry. Staple ears of corn to bulletin board.

Kids can make it!

Enlarge candle pattern onto an 8½" x 11" sheet of white paper. Photocopy candle pattern onto yellow or white construction paper. Have children make their candles by following the directions above. Children can also make Vibunzi (ears of corn) by following directions above. Create a bulletin board display of Vibunzi representing all the children in your class.

Kwanzaa bookmark

Photocopy bookmark onto red or green copier paper.

Foldout table display

Follow "Foldout Table Display" directions on pp. 5–6, using yellow poster board. Staple candles onto the display to make a Kinara. Use authentic artifacts, such as a Mkeka (mat), Kikombe Cha Umaja (unity cup), Mazao (fruits and vegetables) or other African artifacts. Add books on Kwanzaa, African American holidays, African American history, Africa, African and African American folktales, African arts and crafts such as those in the following list.

For display or further reading

Afro-American Folktales: Stories from Black Traditions in the New World. Roger D. Abrahams. New York: Pantheon, 1985. 352 pp.

African American Folktales. Richard Allen Young and Judy Young. Little Rock, AR: August House, 1993. 176p.

The African American Heritage Cookbook. Vanessa Roberts Parham. South Pasadena, CA: Sandcastle, 1993.

African Animal Tales. Rogerio Andrade Barbosa. Volcano, CA: Volcano Press, 1993. 60p.

Celebrating Kwanzaa. Diane Holt-Goldsmith. New York: Holiday, 1993. 32p.

Crafts for Kwanzaa. Kathy Ross. Illustrated by Sharon Lane Holm. Highland Park, NJ: Millbrook Press, 1994. 48p.

Festivals Together. Diana Carey and Judy Large. New York: Hawthorn, 1993. 223p.

Kwanzaa. A.P. Porter. Minneapolis, MN: Lerner Group, 1991. 48p.

Kwanzaa: An African American Celebration of Culture and Cooking. Eric V. Copage. New York: Morrow, 1991. 324p.

Let's Celebrate Kwanzaa: An Activity Book for Young Readers. Helen Davis Thompson. Illustrated by Chris Acemandese Hall. New York: Gumbs and Thomas, 1993. 32p.

Nanta's Lion. Sue MacDonald. New York: Morrow Jr. Books, 1995. 24p.

Seven Candles for Kwanzaa. Andrea Davis Pinkney. New York: Dial, 1993. 32p.

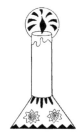 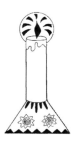  

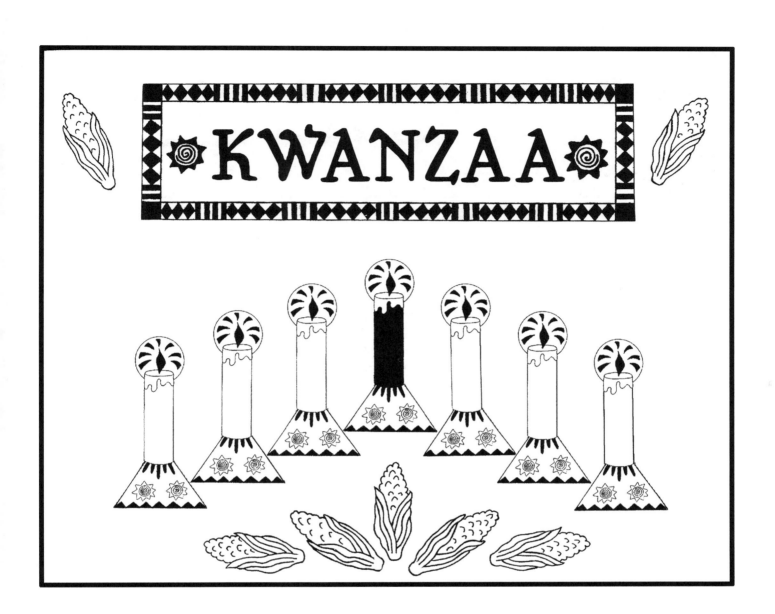

KWANZAA

Animal Antics

11 Horsin' Around

With their graceful, sleek lines and powerful stride, horses have appealed to the imagination of writers and artists since ancient times. The carrousel, or merry-go-round, has been one expression of this love, as a favorite attraction of circuses and amusement parks. To this day, the crowd-pleasing music and fanciful rides make the carrousel a favorite for both young and old.

The first carrousel was made in Europe, probably France, in the late 1700s or early 1800s. It was called a carrousel after an elaborate tournament entertainment given at the court of Henry IV.

Fascinating facts about horses:

> There are more than 150 breeds and types of horses.
>
> The smallest breed is the Fallabella, which comes from Argentina and grows to only 30 inches high at the shoulder.
>
> The largest breed of horse is the Shire, which comes from England and stands more than 68 inches at the shoulder.
>
> Larger breeds can pull loads more than 1,800 pounds.
>
> The fastest horses are the quarter horses and thoroughbreds. Thoroughbreds can run as fast as 45 miles per hour.

Directions for Bulletin Board (p. 55)

BACKGROUND: Cover bulletin board by cutting yellow craft paper to size and stapling to board.

BANNER AND CARROUSEL: Enlarge banner onto white craft paper and outline letters and design with black, wide-tip felt marker. Color carrousel with black, blue, red, green, yellow and pink markers. Cut out carrousel and staple to bulletin board.

POLES: Cut red and white stripe ribbon to make poles for carrousel. Staple ribbon to carrousel.

HORSES: Enlarge horse onto white craft paper and outline with black, wide-tip felt marker. Color horses with black, red, blue, green, yellow and pink with markers. Cut out horses and staple to poles.

Materials you need

- bright yellow craft paper for the background
- white craft paper for the carrousel and horses
- one roll of bright blue scalloped border paper
- black, blue, red, green yellow and pink wide-tip, felt marker
- red and white striped or solid red ribbon (1" wide)

Tools you need

- opaque or overhead projector
- photocopy machine
- scissors
- stapler
- pins

BORDER: Cut scalloped border to fit the perimeter of bulletin board. Staple to bulletin board.

Kids can make it!

Enlarge carrousel horse onto an 8½" x 11" sheet of white paper. Photocopy horses onto white construction paper. Have children color and cut out horses by following directions for horses from above. Tape a red and white striped drinking straw to the back of each horse.

Horse bookmark

Photocopy bookmark onto light blue, yellow or red copier paper.

Foldout table display

Follow "Foldout Table Display" directions on pp. 5–6, using yellow poster board. Staple bright blue scalloped border along bottom of display. Staple horses and poles to display. Exhibit toy carrousel or toy horses, to enhance display. Add books, videos, audiotapes and/or CD-ROMs on horses, carrousels, horse racing, stories about horses from around the world such as those in the following list.

For display or further reading

All the Pretty Horses. Cormac McCathy. New York: Random, 1992.

Billy and Blaze. C.W. Anderson. Cutchogue, NY: Buccaneer, 1992. 56p.

Black Beauty. Anna Sewell.

The Black Stallion. Walter Farley. New York: Random House, 1944. Or any of the titles in Walter Farley's Black Stallion Books series.

The Carrousel. Liz Rozenberg. New York: Putnam, 1995.

Draw 50 Horses. Lee J. Ames. New York: Doubleday, 1984. 64p.

The Girl Who Loved Wild Horses. Paul Goble. Old Tappan, NY: Simon & Schuster, 1993. 32p.

The Horse's Return to America. Smithsonian Wild Heritage Collection. Herman J. Viola. Norwalk, CT: Soundprints, 1995. 32p.

Horses. Elsa Posell. Danbury, CT: Children's Press, 1981. 48p.

Island of Wild Horses. Jack Scott. New York: Putnam, 1978.

King of the Wind. Margurite Henry. Old Tappan, NY: Simon & Schuster, 1991. 224p.

The Lost Merry-Go-Round. Dorothy Lathrop. New York: Macmillan,1943.

Marguerite Henry's Album of Horses: A Pop-Up Book. Marguerite Henry. Illustrated by Ezra Tucker. Old Tappan, NJ: Simon & Schuster, 1993. 32p.

Misty of Chincoteague. Margaret Henry. New York: Scholastic Inc., 1990. 176p.

National Velvet. Enid Bagnold. New York: Morrow Jr. Books, 1985. 207p.

Stormy, Misty's Foal. Margaret Henry. Old Tappan, NJ: Simon & Schuster, 1991.

The World of Horses & Ponies. David Gibbon. CLB Publishing, 1988.

12 Pur-r-r-r-fect Books

They are powerful, frightening, and beautiful—all at the same time. Crowned by authors and artists as the "king of beasts," cats are one of nature's most majestic creatures.

There are three dozen different species of cats, all in the family Felidae. They vary in size from a ten-foot, 600-pound tiger to the smallest domestic house cat weighing only a few pounds. But all cats (felines) share many of the same characteristics.

Each has its own, unique coat. Tigers are known for their stripes. Leopards are famous for their spots. Lions have their regal manes. Other breeds of cat, such as the jaguar, puma, ocelot, cheetah and lynx, have unique patterns as well. Whatever the color or texture, cats keep their coats clean with a built-in scrub brush—a tongue with tiny, hard spikes perfect for picking up loose dirt or hair, or rasping up the last shreds of meat off a bone.

It's uncertain exactly when wild cats were first tamed. There is evidence that the Egyptians lived with tamed cats about 4,000 years ago. The animals were so valued by the Egyptians that they were considered sacred and worshiped in the form of the Goddess Bastet, who protected women, children and the sun's power to ripen crops.

Directions for Bulletin Board (p. 59)

BACKGROUND: Cover bulletin board by cutting yellow craft paper to size and stapling to board.

TITLE: Enlarge "Pur-r-r-r-fect Books" onto bulletin board and outline with red, wide-tip felt marker. Paint in letters with red tempera paint.

BASKET: Enlarge basket onto green craft paper and outline with black, wide-tip felt marker. Cut out basket and cut along dotted line with a craft knife. Staple basket to bulletin board.

CATS: Enlarge cat pattern onto white poster board. Make one large cat and several small kittens. Outline cat patterns with black, wide-tip felt marker. Color cats with brown, gray and orange markers. Cut out each cat and fold along dotted lines. Fold front legs over body and back legs forward. Fold tab behind cat's head and glue to

Materials you need

- bright yellow craft paper for background
- green craft paper for the basket
- white, lightweight poster board for the cats
- pencil
- black, red, brown, gray, blue, green and orange wide-tip felt markers
- red tempera paint
- red yarn
- white glue

Tools you need

- opaque or overhead projector
- photocopy machine
- scissors
- stapler
- pins
- 1" flat-tip brush
- ¼" round-tip brush

front of body. Staple mother cat to bulletin board. Slip kittens into slit in basket. Wind red yarn around kittens and staple in place.

Kids can make it!

Enlarge cat pattern onto an 8½" x 11" sheet of white paper. Photocopy cat pattern onto white construction paper. Have children color and cut out cats. Follow directions above to fold the cats.

Pur-r-r-fect bookmark

Photocopy bookmark onto yellow or pink copier paper.

Foldout table display

Follow "Foldout Table Display" directions on pp. 5–6, using yellow poster board. Staple cats and yarn onto the display. Make a large paper cat and sit on table. Add stuffed cats or cat figures to enhance display. Add books, videos, audiotapes and/or CD-ROMs on domestic and wild cats of all species, fiction and nonfiction such as those in the following list.

For display or further reading

Becoming Your Cat's Best Friend. Bill Gutman. Brookfield, CT: Millbrook Press, 1997.

The Cat in the Hat. Dr. Seuss. New York: Random House, 1957. 72p.

Cat You Better Come Home. Garrison Keillor. Illustrated by Steve Johnson and Lou Fancher. New York: Viking Penguin, 1995.

Cats. Elsa Posell. Danbury, CT: Children's Press, 1983. 48p.

Cats: in from the Wild. Caroline Arnold. Minneapolis: Carolrhoda, 1993.

Draw 50 Cats. Lee J. Ames. New York: Doubleday, 1986.

How to Live with a Calculating Cat. Eric Gurney. New York: Prentice-Hall, 1968.

It's Like This, Cat. Emily Neville. Illustrated by Emil Weiss. New York: Harper, 1963.

Kat Kong. Dav Pilkey. Orlando, FL: Harcourt Brace, 1993.

Millions of Cats. Wanda Gag. New York: Putnam, 1977.

The Mystery of the Missing Cat. Gertrude Chandler Warner. New York: Albert Whitman, 1994.

Puss in Boots. Charles Perrault. Illustrated by Fred Marcellino. New York: Farrar, Straus and Giroux, 1990. 32p.

That Fat Cat. Joanne Barkan. Illustrated by Maggie Swanson. New York: Scholastic, 1992.

Wild Cats. Mary Scott. Illustrated by Roseanna Pistolesi. Mahwah, NJ: Troll Associates, 1992.

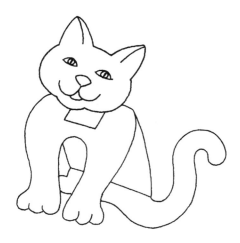

PUR-R-R-RFECT BOOKS

PUR-R-R-R-FECT

BOOKS

13 Hanging Around Bat Caves

Dark, damp and mysterious, caves are naturally a source of intrigue for authors as well as explorers. With their countless twists and turns, caves provide refuge for some and peril for others.

Of the nearly 4,000 species of mammals on Earth, almost one fourth are bats—the only mammals that can fly. Some bats live in trees, but most species of bats live in caves and fly at night. The largest bats, called flying foxes, have a wingspan of over five feet. The smallest bats, known as the Kitti's hog-nosed bats of Thailand, are about the size of a bumblebee.

Throughout history, people have passed on many superstitions and mistaken ideas about bats. For example, most people believe bats are totally blind—hence the expression, "blind as a bat." Actually, all species of bats can see, but their sight is generally poor. Through evolution, they have developed a replacement for sight in the form of a unique "radar" system that they use for their very accurate nocturnal navigations. The bat emits a series of short, high-pitched sounds while in flight. The sounds bounce off approaching objects and the echo helps the bat locate these objects. This is known as "echolocation."

Directions for Bulletin Board (p. 63)

BACKGROUND: Cover bulletin board by cutting black craft paper to size and stapling to board.

STALACTITES AND STALAGMITES: Enlarge stalactites and stalagmites onto bulletin board and outline letters with white chalk. Using a sponge, paint stalactites and stalagmites with light brown tempera paint and let dry. Whip up two parts soap flakes and one part water and add a few drops of brown tempera paint. Dip sponge into fluffy paint and dab it on the stalactites and stalagmites.

TITLE: Enlarge "Hanging Around Bat Caves" onto bulletin board. Outline letters with white chalk and paint in letters with light blue paint.

BATS: Enlarge bats onto a white, 8½" x 11" sheet of paper and outline with a round-tip black felt

Materials you need
- black craft paper for the background
- brown construction paper for bats
- black wide-tip, felt marker
- black round-tip, felt marker
- white chalk
- light brown and light blue tempera paint
- soap flakes

Tools you need
- opaque or overhead projector
- photocopy machine
- scissors
- stapler
- pins
- 1" flat-tip brush
- ¼" round-tip brush
- sponge

marker. Photocopy bats onto brown copier paper. Cut out bats and staple to bulletin board.

Kids can make it!

Enlarge flying bat onto an 8½" x 11" sheet of white paper and outline with a round-tip black felt marker. Photocopy bats onto white construction paper and have children color and cut out a bat. Fold bat in half and punch a hole in the center of the bat. When you open up bat, you will have two parallel holes. Slip an 8" length of yarn or elastic through holes and tie to child's wrist. Have children raise and lower bats to make wings flap.

Bat bookmark

Photocopy bookmark onto brown, red, orange or blue copier paper.

Foldout table display

Follow "Foldout Table Display" directions on pp. 5–6, using black poster board. Paint stalagmites following bulletin boards directions above. Staple bats to display. Add books, videos, audiotapes and/or CD-ROMs on bats, caves, vampires, and Halloween such as those in the following list.

For display or further reading

Bats: Night Fliers. Betsy Maestro. Illustrated by Guilio Maestro. New York: Scholastic, 1995.

Batty Riddles. Katy Hall and Lisa Eisenberg. New York: Dial, 1993.

Caves. Roma Gans. New York: HarperCollins. 1962. 40p.

Count Draculations! Monsters Riddles. Charles Keller. Old Tappan, NJ: Simon & Schuster, 1991.

A First Look at Bats. Millicent Selsa and Joyce Hunt. New York: Walker & Co., 1991.

The Great Ball Game: A Muskogee Story. Joseph Bruchac. New York: Dial, 1994.

Halloween Puzzle Bag. Margaret A. Hartelius. New York: Scholastic.

A Promise to the Sun: An African Story. Tololwa M. Mollel. Boston: Little, Brown, 1992.

Shadows of Night: The Hidden World of the Little Brown Bat. Barbara Bash. San Francisco: Sierra Club, 1993.

Stellaluna. Janell Cannon. Orlando, FL: Harcourt Brace, 1993.

Wempires. Daniel Pinkwater. New York: Macmillan, 1991.

Zoobooks: Bats. Wildlife Education, Ltd., December 1989

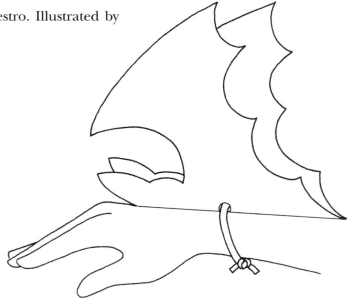

HANGING AROUND BAT CAVES

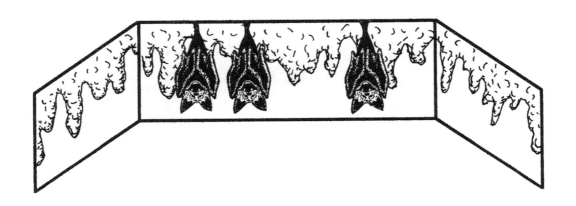

HANGING
AROUND
BAT
CAVES

14 Something to Howl About

Wild dogs—foxes, wolves and coyotes—are a far cry from our friendly, domesticated dog. Yet, all of these dogs evolved from the same carnivores which roamed the earth over 100,000,000 years ago. Today's house pet was first domesticated by the Egyptians over 12,000 years ago.

There are about 35 different species of wild dogs. The largest is the gray wolf, which is found throughout the northern territories of Europe and North America. The gray wolf weighs as much as 150 pounds and stands three feet tall at the shoulders. The smallest wild dog is the fennec, which is found in northern Africa, weighing only five pounds and standing about one foot in height.

Howling is a way for dogs to communicate. When a dog is separated or away from the pack, and vulnerable to attack by predators, he or she instinctively howls. Pack dogs who hear the howling call back, and by communicating back and forth, the separated dog returns to the safety of the pack.

Directions for Bulletin Board (p. 67)

BACKGROUND: Cover bulletin board by cutting black craft paper to size and stapling to board. Enlarge mountains onto purple craft paper and staple to board. Enlarge grass onto green craft paper and staple to board.

COYOTE AND MOON: Enlarge coyote and moon onto light blue poster board. Outline with black, wide-tip felt marker. Cut out coyote and moon. Fold coyote along dotted lines. Fold the front legs over body. Fold tab behind coyote's head and glue to front of body. Staple coyote and moon to bulletin board.

TITLE: Enlarge "Something to Howl About" onto bulletin board and outline with white chalk. Paint in letters with light blue tempera paint.

Materials you need
- black craft paper for the background
- purple or dark blue craft paper for the mountains
- green craft paper for the grass
- light blue, lightweight poster board for the coyote and the moon
- pencil
- black wide-tip felt markers
- white chalk
- light blue tempera paint
- white glue

Tools you need
- opaque or overhead projector
- photocopy machine
- scissors
- stapler
- pins
- 1" flat-tip brush
- ¼" round-tip brush

Kids can make it!

Enlarge coyote pattern onto an 8½" x 11" sheet of white paper. Photocopy coyote pattern onto white construction paper. Have children color and cut out coyotes. Follow directions above to fold the coyotes.

Something to Howl About bookmark

Photocopy bookmark onto light blue, green or purple copier paper.

Foldout table display

Follow "Foldout Table Display" directions on pp. 5–6, using black poster board. Staple coyotes, moon and grass to the display. Make a large paper coyote to sit on table. Add stuffed coyotes, wolves and dog figures to enhance display.

Display books, videos, audiotapes and/or CD-ROMs on "The Wild West," coyotes, wolves, dogs, history of dogs around the world such as those in the following list.

For display or further reading

Amazing Wolves, Dogs, and Foxes. Mary Ling. Photos by Jerry Young. New York: Knopf, 1991.

Aunt Lulu. Daniel Pinkwater. Old Tappan, NJ: Macmillan, 1991.

Call of the Wild. Jack London. New York: Dover, 1989. 64p.

Carl Goes Shopping. Alexandra Day. New York: Farrar, 1989. Also *Carl's Afternoon in the Park* and *Carl's Christmas.*

Coyote: A Trickster Tale from the American Southwest. Gerald McDermot. Orlando, FL: Harcourt Brace, 1994.

Coyote Stories. Robert Rossel, Jr. Chinle, AZ: Roughrock Press.

Dog. Juliet Clutton-Brock. Eyewitness Books. New York: Knopf, 1991.

How Dog Began. Pauline Baynes. New York: Holt, 1985.

Julie of the Wolves. Jean Craighead George. New York: HarperCollins, 1972. 180 p.

Little Red Riding Hood.

Lon Po Po – A Red Riding Hood Story from China. Ed Young. New York: Putnam, 1989. 32p.

Peter and the Wolf Pop-up Book. Sergei Prokofiev. Illustrated by Barbara Cooney. New York: Viking, 1986.

The Tale of Rabbit and Coyote. Tony Johnston. Illustrated by Tomie dePaola. New York: Putnum, 1994.

The Three Little Wolves and the Big Bad Pig. Eugene Trivizas. Illustrated by Helen Oxenbury. Old Tappan, NJ: Macmillan, 1993.

To the Top of the World. Adventures with Artic Wolves. Jim Brandenburg. New York: Walker & Co., 1993. 48pp.

The True Story of the Three Little Pigs. Jon Sciezka. Illustrated by Lane Smith. New York: Viking, 1989. 32p.

Wolves and Coyotes. Jane P. Resnick. Chicago: Kidsbooks, Inc., 1995.

The Ultimate Dog Book. David Taylor. Old Tappan, NJ: Simon & Schuster, 1990.

SOMETHING TO HOWL ABOUT

SOMETHING TO HOWL ABOUT

15 A Whale of a Tale

Whales belong to a group of mammals called cetaceans (see-tay-shunz). There are 75 known species of cetaceans, which are divided into two groups: toothed whales (with teeth) and baleen whales (without teeth).

Whales have the same basic shape as fish, but they differ from fish in important ways. For instance the tail of a whale is horizontal; the tail of a fish is vertical. Fish "breathe" through their gills, absorbing dissolved oxygen from the water. As mammals, whales have lungs and breathe air directly from the atmosphere. Their differences from other mammals are much easier to see—most mammals have four legs and hair. Whales only have a few stiff hairs on their head and no hind legs. Their front legs have evolved into flippers, which helps them to maintain their balance and to steer.

The blue whale is the largest animal that has ever lived, growing up to 100 feet long and weighing more than 100 short tons (200,000 lbs.). The sperm whale can hold its breath for as long as 75 minutes at a time. Whales have very poor eyesight and no sense of smell, relying primarily on their hearing to provide them with information about their surroundings.

Directions for Bulletin Board (p. 71)

BACKGROUND: Cover bulletin board by cutting light blue craft paper to size and stapling to board.

WAVES: Enlarge waves onto dark blue craft paper the same width as bulletin board. Outline waves with white chalk and cut out. Mix a few drops of green tempera paint into white tempera paint. Sponge paint onto tops of waves. Let dry, then cut out waves. Staple waves to board leaving unstapled at the top of bottom row of waves.

WHALES: Enlarge whales onto gray craft paper and outline with black, wide-tip felt marker. Cut out whales, slip between waves and staple to bulletin board.

SPOUT AND TITLE: Enlarge spout and "A Whale of a Tale" onto white craft paper. Outline spout

Materials you need
- light blue craft paper for the background
- dark blue craft paper for the waves
- gray craft paper for the whales
- white craft paper for the spout
- pencil
- red and black wide-tip felt marker
- white and green tempera paint
- white chalk

Tools you need
- opaque or overhead projector
- photocopy machine
- scissors
- stapler
- pins
- sponge

with black, wide-tip felt marker and "A Whale of a Tale" with red, wide-tip felt marker. Fill in letters with red, wide-tip felt marker. Staple spout to bulletin board.

Kids can make it!

Enlarge whale hat onto an 8½" x 11" sheet of white paper. Photocopy hats onto white construction paper and have children color and cut out hats. Punch a hole on each end of hat and tie a 12" length of yarn through each hole. Tie hats onto children's heads.

A Whale of a Tale bookmark

Photocopy bookmark onto light blue copier paper.

Foldout table display

Follow "Foldout Table Display" directions on pp. 5–6, using light blue poster board. Staple waves and whale to board. Add stuffed whales, dolphins, fish and other sea creatures, shells, starfish and netting to enhance display. Add books, videos, audio tapes and/or CD-ROMs on the sea, whales, oceans, sea creatures, mermaids and oceanography such as those in the following list.

For display or further reading

Arctic Whales and Whaling. Bobbie Kalman and Ken Fairis. New York: Crabtree, 1988.

Do the Whales Still Sing? Dianne Hofmeyr. Illustrated by Jude Daly. New York: Dial, 1995.

Humphrey the Lost Whale: A True Story. Wendy Tokunda and Richard Hall. Illustrated by Hanako Wakiyama. Torrance, CA: Heian, 1986.

John Tabor's Ride. Edward C. Day. Illustrated by Dirk Zimmer. New York: Knopf, 1989. 32 pp.

Killer Whales. Dorothy Hinshaw Patent. New York: Holiday, 1993.

Little Mermaid. Hans Christian Andersen. Kansas City, MO: Andrews & McMeel, 1992. 32p.

The Mermaid and the Whale. George McHargue.

Moby Dick. Herman Melville. Mahwah, NJ: Troll, 1988. 48pp.

The Seal Oil Lamp. Dale DeArmond. San Francisco: Sierra Club, 1988.

The Seashell Song. Susie Jenkin-Pearce. Illustrated by Claire Fletcher. New York: Lothrop, 1993.

Sukey and the Mermaid. Robert San Souci. Illustrated by Brian Pinkney. Old Tappan, NJ: Simon & Schuster Childrens, 1992. 32p.

Whale Brother. Barbara Steiner. New York: Walker & Co., 1988.

Whale Song. Tony Johnston. Illustrated by Ed Young. New York: Putnam, 1987.

The Whale's Song. Dyan Sheldon. Illustrated by Gary Blythe. New York: Dial, 1991. 32p.

Whales, the Nomads of the Sea. Helen Roney Sattler. Illustrated by Jean Day Zallinger. New York: Lothrop, 1987. 128 pp.

A WHALE OF
A TALE

A WHALE OF
A TALE

16 Book Hogs

People who see hogs wallowing in mud often consider them dirty and stupid. Yet hogs actually keep themselves quite clean and are considered to be one of the most intelligent of all animals.

The hog and pig belong to the same family, Suidae. Six million years ago, wild hogs roamed throughout Europe and other parts of the world. People in China began taming hogs about 9,000 years ago, during the Stone Age; and about a thousand years later in Europe. Christopher Columbus brought hogs with him to North and South America in the early 1500s.

Fascinating hog facts:

    Hogs gain an average of 1½ pounds per day, every day.
    Male hogs reach an average weight of 350–500 pounds.

    There are about 90 different breeds of hogs today

    Hog hair or "bristles" are used to make hair brushes

    Hogs produce a chemical, ACTH, which can used by
    humans to help manage diabetes

Directions for Bulletin Board (p. 75)

BACKGROUND: Cover bulletin board by cutting light blue craft paper to size and stapling to board. Cover the bottom third of bulletin board by cutting brown craft paper the same width as bulletin board. Cut top of brown craft paper to look like a wavy line. Staple to bulletin board.

BORDER: Cut pink scalloped paper to fit the perimeter of bulletin board. Staple to board.

TITLE: Enlarge "Book Hogs" onto bulletin board. Outline letters with brown, wide-tip felt markers and paint in letters with brown tempera paint.

HOGS: Enlarge hogs onto pink craft paper and outline with black, wide-tip felt marker. Cut out hogs and staple to bulletin board.

Materials you need
- light blue craft paper for the background
- brown craft paper for the mud
- pink craft paper for the pigs
- 1 roll pink scalloped paper
- pencil
- black and brown wide-tip, felt marker
- brown tempera paint

Tools you need
- opaque or overhead projector
- photocopy machine
- scissors
- stapler
- pins
- 1" flat-tip brush
- ¼" round-tip brush

Kids can make it!

Enlarge hog hat onto a white, 8½" x 11" sheet of paper. Photocopy hats onto white construction paper. Have children color and cut out hats. Punch a hole on each end of hat and tie a 12" length of yarn through each hole. Tie hats onto children's heads.

Book Hogs bookmark

Photocopy bookmark onto pink or light blue copier paper.

Foldout table display

Follow "Foldout Table Display" directions on pp. 5–6, using light blue poster board. Staple brown paper onto board for mud. Staple hogs onto board. Add stuffed pigs or pig figures to enhance display. Add books, videos, audiotapes and/or CD-ROMs on pigs, pig stories, farms, farm animals such as those in the following list.

For display or further reading

All Kinds of Farms. Ann Larkin Hansen. Minneapolis: Abdo & Daughters, 1996. Also *Crops on the Farm* and *Seasons of the Farm.*

The Book of Pigericks: Pig Limericks. Arnold Lobel. New York: HarperCollins, 1983.

Color Farm. Lois Ehlert. New York: Lippincott, 1990.

EIEIO: The Story of Old MacDonald, Who Had a Farm. Gus Clarke. New York: Lothrop, 1993.

Juan Bobo and the Pig: A Puerto Rican Folktale. Felix Pitre. Illustrated by Christy Hale. New York: Lodestar, 1993.

Hanna's Hog. Jim Aylesworth. Illustrated by Glen Rounds. New York: Atheneum, 1988.

The Happy Hedgehog Band. Martin Waddell. Illustrated by Jill Barton. Cambridge, MA: Candlewick Press, 1992.

Hog-Eye. Susan Meddaugh. Boston: Houghton Mifflin, 1995.

Parents in the Pig Pen, Pigs in the Tub. Amy Ehrlich. New York: Dial, 1993.

Pig Pig Goes to Camp. David McPhail. New York: Dutton, 1983.

Piggies. Don and Audrey Wood. Illustrated by Don Wood. Orlando, FL: Harcourt Brace Jovanovich, 1991.

Pigs Aplenty, Pigs Galore! David McPail. New York: Dutton, 1993.

Pigs from A to Z. Arthur Geisert. Boston: Houghton Mifflin, 1986.

The Pig's Wedding. Helme Heine. New York: McElderry, 1979.

Pigsty. Mark Teague. New York: Scholastic Inc., 1994.

Small Pig. Arnold Lobel. New York: HarperCollins., 1988.

Two Crazy Pigs. Karen Berman Nagel. Illustrated by Brian Schatell. New York: Scholastic Inc., 1992.

Wibbly Pig (series). Mick Inkpen. Racine, WI: Western, 1995.

BOOK HOGS

17 Dragon Tales

Dragons are curious creatures, with a legendary history in literature and the arts. As mythical beasts in the folklore of many European and Asian cultures, dragons are usually large, lizard-like animals that breathe fire and have long, scaly tails.

In Europe, dragons are traditionally represented as ferocious beasts, the embodiment of evil. The tale of Saint George, a Christian martyr and patron saint of England, and his encounter with a dragon is one popular example. A pagan town in Libya had fallen victim to a dragon (representing the devil). The inhabitants tried to placate the dragon by offering sheep; when that didn't work, they began offering members of their community. The king's daughter had been chosen as the next sacrifice. However, George arrived, killed the dragon, and converted the community of Christianity. In England this victory is celebrated as George's Feast on April 23.

In Asia, dragons are portrayed as friendly creatures that ensure good luck and wealth. In China, for instance, the dragon is the center of festivity and celebration. The traditional New Year's Day parade includes groups of dancers who wind through the streets wearing large, colorful dragon costumes. For those who believe, the power of the dragon brings the rainfall needed for the next year's harvest. The Dragon Dance is used to expel devils and bring people good luck in the new year.

Directions for Bulletin Board (p. 79)

BACKGROUND: Cover bulletin board by cutting light blue craft paper to size and stapling to board.

TITLE: Enlarge "Dragon Tales" onto bulletin board and outline letters with red, wide-tip felt marker. Paint in letters with red tempera paint.

DRAGON: Enlarge dragon onto green craft paper and outline with black, wide-tip felt marker. Cut out dragon and staple to bulletin board. Cut out tongue and eye from red construction paper and glue onto dragon. Trace scale pattern onto a stack of tissue paper and cut out scales. Glue scales onto dragon in alternating colors.

Kids can make it!

Enlarge dragon onto an 8½" x 11" sheet of white paper. Photocopy dragons onto white construc-

Materials you need
- light blue craft paper for the background
- green craft paper for the dragon
- blue, green and purple tissue paper
- red construction paper
- red, blue and black wide-tip, felt marker
- pencil
- white glue
- red tempera paint

Tools you need
- opaque or overhead projector
- photocopy machine
- scissors
- stapler
- pins
- 1" flat-tip brush
- ¼" round-tip brush

tion paper and have children color dragon and glue on dried split peas for the scales.

Dragon Tales bookmark

Photocopy bookmark onto light blue, green or purple copier paper.

Foldout table display

Follow "Foldout Table Display" directions on pp. 6–7, using light blue poster board. Staple dragon onto board. Add stuffed dragons or dragon figures, castles, knights or princesses to enhance display.

Display books, videos, audio tapes and/or CD-ROMs on dragons, knights, chivalry, medieval times, the Crusades, King Arthur, Camelot and dragon stories from around the world such as those in the following list.

For display or further reading

The Adventures of King Midas. Lynne Reid Banks. Illustrated by Joseph A. Smith. New York: Morrow, 1992.

The Book of Dragons. Michael Hague. New York: Morrow Jr. Books, 1995.

The Dragon Nanny. C.L. E. Martin. Old Tappan, NJ: Simon & Schuster, 1988.

Dragon Song. Anne McCaffrey. New York: Atheneum, 1976.

Dragondrums. Anne McCaffrey. New York: Bantam, 1980.

Dragons–A Natural History. Dr. Karl Shuker. Old Tappan, NJ: Simon & Schuster, 1995.

The Dragons Are Singing Tonight. Jack Prelutsky. Illustrated by Peter Sis. New York: Greenwillow, 1993.

Dragons in the Waters. Madeleine L'Engle. New York: Dell, 1982.

Dragons: Truth, Myth, and Legend. David Passes. Illustrated by Wayne Anderson. Racine, WI: Artists & Writers Guild, 1993.

Dragonsinger. Anne McCaffrey. New York: Atheneum, 1977.

Eric Carle's Dragons, Dragons, Dragons & Other Creatures That Never Were. Laura Whipple. Illustrated by Eric Carle. New York: Philomel, 1991.

Greg Hildebrandt's Book of Three-Dimensional Dragons. Boston: Little, Brown, 1994.

Jeremy Thatcher, Dragon Hatcher. Bruce Coville. Illustrated by Gary A. Lippincott. Orlando, FL: Harcourt Brace.

Knights of the Kitchen Table. Jon Scieszka. Illustrated by Lane Smith. New York: Viking, 1991.

My Father's Dragon. Ruth Gannett. New York: Knopf, 1987.

The Library Dragon. Carmen Agra Deedy. Atlanta, GA: Peachtree, 1994.

The Minstrel and the Dragon Pup. Rosemary Sutcliff. Illustrated by Emma Chichester Clark. Cambridge, MA: Candlewick Press, 1993.

Saint George and the Dragon. Margaret Hodges. Illustrated by Trina Schart Hyman. Boston: Little, Brown, 1984.

The Truth about Dragons. Rhoda Blumberg. Illustrated by Murray Tinkleman. New York: Four Winds, 1980.

DRAGON
TALES

18 Leaping Library Books

Whether it's a "frog prince" or a mythical toad taking a "wild ride," frogs and toads have been the source of legend and superstition. One myth says that frogs fall from the sky during a rain. In fact, many species that live underground leave their burrows during or shortly after a rainstorm. Because people seldom see these frogs, stories have been made up to explain their sudden appearance.

The first frogs appeared on earth about 180 million years ago. About 2,700 species of frogs and toads have developed from these early ancestors. The Goliath frog of west-central Africa is the largest species, measuring nearly 12" in length. The smallest species grow only ½" long.

What's the difference between a frog and a toad? True toads have a broader, flatter body and darker, drier skin than do most true frogs. Toads are also commonly covered with warts. True frogs have smooth skin. Toads generally live on land, while most true frogs live on, in and near water.

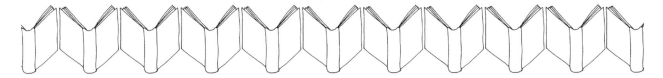

Directions for Bulletin Board (p. 83)

BACKGROUND: Cover bulletin board by cutting yellow craft paper to size and stapling to board. Cover bottom third of bulletin board by cutting light blue craft paper to the same width and stapling to board.

TITLE: Enlarge "Leaping Library Books" onto bulletin board and outline letters with green, wide-tip marker. Paint in letters with green tempera paint.

FROGS: Enlarge frog pattern onto green craft paper and outline with black, wide-tip felt marker. Cut out frog pattern and accordion-fold legs and arms. Glue arms and legs to back of frog. Staple frogs to bulletin board.

LILLY PADS, FLOWERS AND BOOKS: Enlarge lily pad onto green craft paper and outline with

Materials you need

- yellow craft paper for the background
- light blue craft paper for the water
- green craft paper for the frogs and lily pads
- pink craft paper for the books and flowers
- 1 roll pink scalloped border paper
- black and green wide-tip, felt marker
- green tempera paint
- white glue

Tools you need

- opaque or overhead projector
- photocopy machine
- scissors
- stapler
- pins
- 1" flat-tip brush
- ¼" round-tip brush

black-wide tip felt marker. Cut out lily pads and staple to board. Enlarge flower and book onto pink craft paper and outline with black, wide-tip felt marker. Cut out flowers and glue onto lily pads. Cut out books and glue to frog's hands.

BORDER: Cut scalloped border to fit perimeter of bulletin board. Staple to bulletin board.

Kids can make it!

Enlarge frog pattern and book onto an 8½" x 11" sheet of white paper. Photocopy frog pattern and book onto white construction paper and have children color and cut out frogs and books. Follow directions on how to assemble frogs from above.

Leaping Library bookmark

Photocopy bookmark onto green, pink or light blue copier paper.

Foldout table display

Follow "Foldout Table Display" directions on pp. 5–6, using light blue poster board. Staple frogs and lily pads onto the display. Put a terrarium of frogs on display. Add stuffed frogs or frog figures to enhance display.

Display books, videos, audiotapes and/or CD-ROMs on frogs, lily ponds, amphibians such as those in the following list.

For display or further reading

Commander Toad (series). Jane Yolen. Illustrated by Bruce Degen. New York: Putnam, 1980–1987.

The Complete Frog: A Guide for the Very Young Naturalist. Elizabeth A. Lacey. Illustrated by Christopher Santoro. New York: Lothrop, 1989.

Drawing from Nature. Jim Arnosky. New York: Lothrop, 1987.

An Extraordinary Egg. Leo Lionni. New York: Knopf, 1994.

The Frog Prince. Retold by Edith H. Tarcov. Illustrated by James Marshall. New York: Scholastic Inc., 1974.

The Frog Prince Continued. Jon Scieszka. Paintings by Steve Johnson. New York: Puffin, 1994.

Frog Went A-Courtin'. John Langstaff. Pictures by Feodor Rojankovsky. Orlando FL: Harcourt Brace, 1955.

Frog and Toad Are Friends. Arnold Lobel. New York: Harper, 1970.

Frogs and Toads. Helen Riley. New York: Thomson Learning, 1993.

Frogs in Clogs. Sheila White Samton. New York: Crown, 1995.

Green Wilma. Ted Arnold. New York: Dial Books, 1993.

The Magic School Bus Hops Home. Patricia Relf. New York: Scholastic Inc., 1995.

Slippery Babies: Young Frogs, Toads, and Salamanders. Ginny Johnston and Judy Cutchins. New York: Morrow, 1991.

The Wind in the Willows. Kenneth Grahame.

LEAPING LIBRARY BOOKS

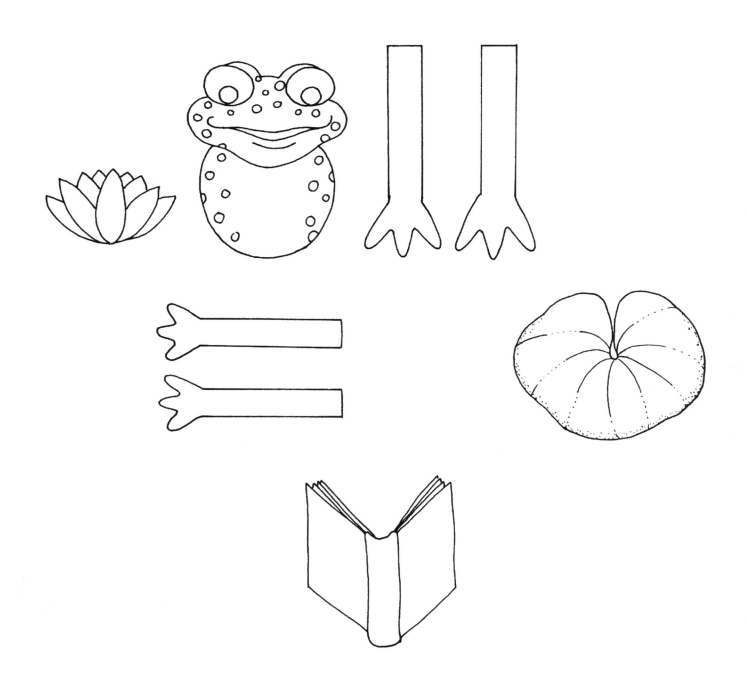

LEAPING
LIBRARY
BOOKS

19 Spin a Story

Literature has not really been fair to the spider. From the stories we read, it would seem that this eight-legged creature, or arachnid, is one of the deadliest known to humankind. After all, every spider can bite and almost every spider's bite contains some form of poison. Yet, of the 35,000 known species of spiders, only about a dozen are harmful or deadly to people.

The largest spider, the tarantula, is about ten inches across, including its legs. Despite their eerie look, most tarantulas are harmless to humans. The smallest spiders are smaller than the head of a pin. Spiders are actually helpful to humankind. For example, spiders kill grasshoppers and locusts, which are known to destroy crops; they also eat flies and mosquitoes, which carry diseases; and spiders help control the population of mice, birds, lizards, frogs and fish. Most female spiders are larger and stronger than their male partners—and, in many cases, these females will eat the males when they are no longer useful.

One of the most recognized features of a spider is its web. In fact, spiders can be classified according to the kind of webs they weave: radial, triangular, orb, platform, sheet-form, bowl-and-doily, labyrinth, and loosely woven. If you take a closer look, the silk strands of the web are actually shaped in the form of a beaded necklace. These can be used for "flying" as well as weaving.

Directions for Bulletin Board (p. 87)

BACKGROUND: Cover bulletin board by cutting orange craft paper to size and stapling to board.

WEB: Stretch yarn pieces from corner to corner, top to bottom and side to side—all intersecting in the center of the board. Staple yarn pieces to board as you go. Tie yarn to center of web, then from one piece of yarn to the other to form a spiral.

BANNER: Enlarge banner onto green craft paper. Outline letters and fill in with black, wide-tip felt marker. Staple banner to bulletin board.

SPIDERS: Enlarge spider pattern onto black craft paper and outline with white colored pencil. Cut out spider. Accordion-fold spider legs. Glue four sections of spider body together at the top.

Materials you need
- orange craft paper for the background
- black craft paper for the spiders
- bright green craft paper for the banner
- white construction paper for eyes
- pencil
- black wide-tip, felt marker
- black round-tip, felt marker
- white glue
- white colored pencil

Tools you need
- opaque or overhead projector
- photocopy machine
- scissors
- stapler
- pins

Glue spider body to legs. Draw eyes onto white construction paper with black, round-tip felt marker. Cut out eyes and glue to spider's body. Staple spiders to bulletin board.

Kids can make it!

Enlarge spider pattern onto an 8½" x 11" sheet of white paper. Photocopy spider pattern onto white construction paper and have children color and cut out spiders. Follow assembly instructions from above. Spiders can be suspended from ceiling with string and hung around the room.

Spider bookmark

Photocopy bookmark onto green, orange or red copier paper.

Foldout table display

Follow "Foldout Table Display" directions on pp. 5–6, using orange or green poster board. Staple yarn and spiders onto display. Place a terrarium with spiders on the table. Add books, videos, audiotapes and/or CD-ROMs on spiders, Halloween, spider stories such as those in the following list.

For display or further reading

Anansi and the Talking Melon. Eric Kimmel. Illustrated by Janet Stevens. New York: Holiday House, 1994. Also **Anansi Goes Fishing** and **Anansi and the Moss-Covered Rock.**

Charlotte's Web. E.B. White. New York: HarperCollins, 1952.

The Fascinating World of Spiders. Maria Julivert. Illustrated by Marcel Studios. Hauppauge, NY: Barrons, 1992.

Favorite Scary Stories of American Children. Richard Young and Judy Dockrey Young. Illustrated by Wendell E. Hall. Little Rock, AR: August House, 1990.

The Itsy Bitsy Spider. Iza Trapani. Dallas, TX: Whispering Coyote Press, 1993.

Scary Stories e: More Tales to Chill Your Bones. Alvin Schwartz. New York: HarperCollins, 1991. Also *Scary Stories to Tell in the Dark* and *More Scary Stories to Tell in the Dark.*

Spider on the Floor. Raffi. Words and music by Bill Russell. New York: Crown, 1993.

Miss Spider's Tea Party. David Kirk. New York: Scholastic Inc., 1994.

Miss Spider's Wedding. David Kirk. New York: Scholastic Inc., 1995.

The Roly-Poly Spider. Jill Sardegna. Illustrated by Tedd Arnold. New York: Scholastic Inc., 1994.

Seven Spiders Spinning. Gregory Maguire. Boston: Houghton Mifflin, 1994.

The Very Busy Spider. Eric Carle. New York: Putnam, 1989.

20 Herd Any Good Stories Lately?

The elephant is the largest animal on land. Its size alone has fascinated writers and has been the subject of both fiction and nonfiction. There are two different kinds of elephants: the African and Asiatic (also known as Indian) elephant. The African elephant, which is native only to Africa, is larger and fiercer than its counterpart, with males standing about eleven feet at the shoulder and weighing about six short tons (4,800 lbs.). Asiatic elephants are native to both Asia and India. Males stand about nine to ten and a half feet at the shoulder and weigh about four short tons (3,600 lbs.).

Fascinating facts about elephants:

Elephant skin is as much as 1½" thick and can weigh as much as a short ton (1,800 lb.)

Elephants are not slow. They can run as fast as 25 miles per hour when startled or a steady pace of ten miles an hour when marching

Elephants touch trunks as a greeting, much like people shake hands

Elephants love water and are considered excellent swimmers

A wild African elephant eats over 750 pounds of food per day and drinks over 40 gallons of water

Directions for Bulletin Board (p. 91)

BACKGROUND: Cover bulletin board by cutting pink craft paper to size and stapling to board.

TITLE: Enlarge "Herd Any Good Stories Lately" onto bulletin board. Outline letters with green, wide-tip felt markers and paint in letters with green paint.

GRASS: Cut a 12"-wide section of green craft paper the same width as bulletin board. Cut top edge of green craft paper to look like blades of grass. Staple green craft paper to bulletin board.

ELEPHANTS: Enlarge elephants onto gray craft paper and outline with black, wide-tip felt marker. Cut out elephants and staple to bulletin board.

Materials you need
- pink craft paper for the background
- gray craft paper for elephants
- green craft paper for the grass
- black and green wide-tip felt marker
- pencil
- green tempera paint

Tools you need
- opaque or overhead projector
- photocopy machine
- scissors
- stapler
- pins
- 1" flat-tip brush
- ¼" round-tip brush

Kids can make it!

Enlarge each elephant ear and trunk onto a separate 8½" x 11" sheet of white paper. Photocopy elephant ears and trunk onto white construction paper and have children color and cut out both the ears and the trunk. Fold tabs back on elephant ears and glue to a paper headband. Glue trunk to inside of headband and let drop over front of headband.

Elephant bookmark

Photocopy bookmark onto gray, pink or green copier paper.

Foldout Table Display

Follow "Foldout Table Display" directions on pp. 5–6, using pink or light blue poster board. Staple elephants and grass onto the display. Exhibit stuffed elephants or elephant figures to enhance display. Add books, videos, audiotapes and/or CD-ROMs on elephants, circus, and the jungle such as those in the following list.

For display or further reading

Barbar the Magician. Laurent De Brunhoff. New York: Random House, 1980.

The Blind Men and the Elephant. Karen Backstein.

Illustrated by Annie Mitra. New York: Scholastic Inc., 1992.

Circus. Lois Ehlert. New York: HarperCollins, 1992.

Dumbo. Teddy Slater. Illustrated by Ron Dias and Annie Guenther. Racine, WI: Golden Books, 1988.

The Elephant at the Waldorf. Anne Miranda. Illustrated by Don Vanderbeek. Mahwah, NJ: Bridgewater Books, 1995.

The Elephant's Child. Rudyard Kipling. Illustrated by Tim Raglin. New York: Harcourt Brace, 1986.

Elephants. Elsa Posell. Danbury, CT: Children's Press, 1982.

Horton Hears a Who! Dr. Seuss. New York: Random House, 1954.

17 Kings and 42 Elephants. Margaret Mahy. New York: Dial, 1987.

The Right Number of Elephants. Jeff Sheppard. Illustrated by Felica Bond. New York: HarperCollins, 1993. (big book).

Seven Blind Mice. Ed Young. New York: Philomel, 1992.

Zoobooks: Elephants. Wildlife Education, Ltd., 1994.

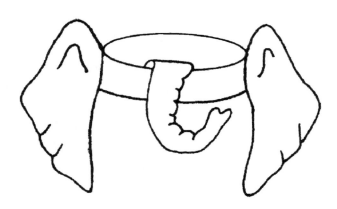

HERD ANY GOOD STORIES LATELY?

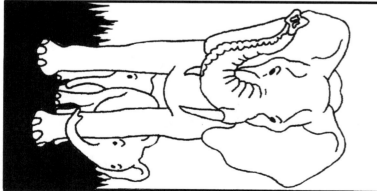

HERD ANY GOOD STORIES LATELY?